Dear Pa...
A delight...

With A Smile And A Song

by
Kelly Richards

With love

Kelly ×

With A Smile And A Song

by
Kelly Richards
dedicated to my "Three Little Angels"

Publisher
Mediaworld PR Ltd
Best Books Online

Preface

"With A Smile And A Song"

I never thought in a hundred years that I would be writing a book. Well that is not totally true. When I was about nine years old, I did see myself as somewhat of an author, and I convinced myself that by the age of ten I would have written my first novel, and be half way to being acclaimed as the world's (nothing by halves) greatest writer. As I recall I had no idea what the novel's story line would be, but I did know that the first line of this book would be "I was alone that night, but not afraid..." that was it. I am sure you have realised by now that I am not the world's greatest author, nor ever likely to be!! I was tempted for old time's sake to start off this biography with my famous opening, but you will be glad to know I have not!

So, I think we can safely establish that I am not a Dickens, Shakespeare (although we do share the same birthday) or Ruth Rendell, but hopefully I have been able to put my memories, along with accurate accounts of my aunt's life and times during her sixty years in show business, onto paper.

My aim and wish is for this biography to be easy to read and follow, and most of all to be interesting. There are many insights into her personal life, also stories of her life that have never before, as far as I am aware, been shared.

It has taken ten years for me to finally decide to write this biography. I must admit I have been very tempted to use a ghostwriter, but my gut feeling was that no matter how good the ghostwriter was, their interpretations of my memories would not be recorded with the same feeling as mine have, as it would all be second-hand.

I knew, and loved Anne Shelton. We were very close from my early childhood and remained so until her sudden death in 1994. It seems fitting that I am the one to complete this final tribute to such a wonderful lady.

It is not my intention to bore you with "a little bit about the author" as it is not me that you, the reader, wants to know about, but I would like to say that not a day goes by that I do not think about my aunt and how I miss her wonderful smile, warm comforting voice, words of wisdom, and most of all those lovely big hugs.

She was greatly loved and over the years since her death I have been overwhelmed by the tributes and correspondence that I have received from her fans, that are still many. Due to this amazing following that she still has, I decided to hand the last chapter of this book over to the fans, shall we call it "The People's Tribute". I hope you find the memories that have been recorded by these wonderful people as interesting and as touching as I have.

Finally there is my 'thank you' list. Firstly to Di Tucker who has always given me so much support and has been responsible for collating and producing all the photographs in the biography. Big thanks also to Jim Woolley, my Guru, for without his incredible memory and his comprehensive knowledge of my aunt's early career I would have been lost. Neville Sumpter who has written the extensive and complete discography of Anne's recordings, he must have worked so hard, for this I am most grateful.

The last person that I would like to mention is a very talented artist by the name of Peter Miller. I was so impressed with the two pictures that he sent me depicting Air Force scenes of WW2 that I have included them in the picture section. Should anyone want more information about Peter's work, contact me and I will be happy to put you in touch with him.

All that remains is for me to thank you for buying this book, and to wish you all good health, happiness and peace throughout your lives.

Chapter One

Patricia Jacqueline Sibley

Patricia Jacqueline Sibley born 10th November in the year, as she used to say, "1900 and frozen to death."

For those of you who don't know, perhaps I should mention that Patty Sibley, as she was known from birth, grew up to be Anne Shelton, the World War II Forces Favourite.

My intention is not to confuse the readers, but you will see as you progress through the following chapters, that I refer to my late aunt sometimes as Anne and other times as Patty. The reason for this is that this biography is about the life of one of Britain's greatest singers, my Aunt Anne, it is also about a truly loving, kind, amazing woman, my Aunt Patty. So the thing that you need to remember as we go through the account of her life together is Patty and Anne are one and the same.

As I have already mentioned, Patty was born 10th November at 39 Coleman Road, Camberwell, London, to William and Lammatana Sibley. She was their third child. A blonde, curly haired baby with, I am told, the biggest of blue eyes. She had an elder brother and sister. Her brother Bill, named after their father, was the eldest, he was born on 25th March 1908 at 33 Whitehorse Road, Eastham, London. Her elder sister Eileen was born 31st May 1916, also at Eastham. Eileen, or Eisie as she was called by the family, was my mother. Then on 8th December 1936 came Jo (Josie) who was one of twins, the other child sadly was stillborn. Josie was also born at Coleman Road, Camberwell.

Patty always used to say how she remembered being so excited when her mother was expecting her fourth child. She was so happy when Josie was born, as she was convinced, and told the whole family that the baby was her Christmas present. Patty and Josie had a very special relationship from the very start and it was one that they maintained all through their lives. They were as close as close could be, right up until Jo's death in 1991.

Her parents Bill and Lamma were ordinary Eastenders. Bill worked for the Commercial Cable Company in the City of London, and Lamma, who was born in Barking, Essex, was a housewife and mother. Lamma's maiden name was Bower. Her family was of Spanish origin, when her great grandparents arrived in England their name was Forwarda, which was changed for whatever reason to Forward. Bill Sibley's roots were from Ireland, so the blood flowing through the young Sibleys' veins was of an Irish/Spanish mix, probably accounting for the family's fiery tempers and for their loving, close relationships, it would also account for their staunch Catholic beliefs.

The younger Sibleys were inseparable. Patty took on the self-inflicted 'charge' of Josie. She took care of her, shared her sweets with her and became a little mother hen. She used to get her ready for bed and school, combed her long hair and generally looked out for her. Despite the age difference they were close friends as well as sisters.

The first school Patty attended was the Convent of Mercy in Camberwell, London. She was a good pupil, never in trouble, always did as she was told, and showed her compassionate, caring personality even at that early age. She would always befriend those girls at school who were either picked on or bullied. She hated injustice, a trait that carried on all through her life.

Having attended a convent myself, I know how strict and intimidating the nuns can be and I would imagine it was even worse in those days. Her best friend was Marcel Moneypenny. I wonder if she is still alive today?

The family moved to 9 Ewlme Road, Forest Hill, South East London. Patty then attended the Sacred Heart Convent in Forest Hill. She was an average scholar, her favourite subject being history. It was obvious from an early age that she had no desire to

4

be another Einstein. She also enjoyed netball, playing for the school team.

Always singing at home, or wherever she was, she decided that she would very much like to join the school choir. This she did, but it was soon after joining that Patricia was asked to leave, as she sang in too low a key! I wonder if the teacher that threw her out of the choir ever followed her career?

My grandmother ruled the children (and my granddad come to that) with a rod of iron. She was the typical Catholic mother who was the centre of the family. I remember as a child that my Nan (or Nanshe as I called her) most certainly had the view a child should be seen and not heard, if I was ever being naughty she only had to look at me and I would freeze. I believe this was also the case with her own children. I must say as a child my Nan did frighten me and when she shouted, everyone ran including Chang the family dog who was a beautiful ginger Chow. Granddad on the other hand was kind, calm and very under the thumb. I think he was the one the children went to for their love and comfort, Nan was the disciplinarian.

Being older, Eileen and Bill had more freedom and were out more, which left Patty and Josie as allies at home. All through their lives they always wanted to please their mother, none of the children ever answered back, even when they became adults they still showed that respect unlike, unfortunately, some youths of today.

Patty's extraordinary talent showed from an early age. She had the most amazing voice, so powerful for one so young. I would like to relate a story she told me several times and one I never tired of hearing. She was about three or four, the family were travelling on a bus going over Tower Bridge, when the blonde haired little Sibley girl, dressed in a red velvet coat amazed the family, and the other passengers, by jumping up to attention and singing very loudly "God Bless the Prince of Walesssss". I believe even then, all were completely amazed by her powerful, perfectly pitched deliverance.

Life was happy for the Sibleys. Lamma had a sister called

Louise, Lou for short. The two sisters spent a lot of time together, so the Sibley children not only had a mother around to care for them but also a doting aunt, of whom they were all very fond. Lamma and Lou also had good voices, so many an afternoon was spent with Lamma on the piano, Aunty Lou and the girls (Patty and Jo) singing along, what fun they must have had, it is, they say, in the genes. I don't know what went wrong with Bill and Eileen's genes, but neither of them could sing a note, both had voices as flat as pancakes. In later life when we were at home as a family, sometimes my mum, Eileen, would sing along to a song that might be playing on the radio, and my sister and I would say, "Don't sing mum you are out of tune." Mum would reply, "I know, sorry I just can't sing," and if ever Aunty Patty was at our house she would spring to her defence and say; "yes you can Eileen, let's sing along together." She would then sing along with mum whose voice seemed to magically be transformed and be in tune. That was the type of person Patty was, she always stood up for anyone who was being made to feel inadequate, or being picked on, or maybe ridiculed. Not that we intentionally ever did that to mum!

Bill Junior went to work with his father in the Cable Company, Eileen went to work in a local butcher's shop in Camberwell, which was one of several owned by a family called Richards. George, one of the four sons, ran this business. Eileen started dating George and later went on to marry him. (George was my dad)

Lamma was a wonderful cook. As was often the case in those days, all the fare for the table was home produced. Bread, cakes, biscuits, pies, all to die for. One source of protein that was never on the menu for Patty was cheese. From an early age she had an intolerance, although strangely enough not to other dairy products. She used to tell me it sent her green, I must confess I was never witness to this, but it did make her very poorly if eaten.

Digressing slightly, I remember a meal that my Nan Lamma, used to serve regularly on a Saturday when the whole family would meet up for lunch. It was these wonderful boiled sausages that had been cooked with onions and vegetables, then served with mashed potato and a delicious thick white gravy. I have never tasted anything like it since, and have never been able to conjure up the dish myself. Does anyone know how she made that gravy?

Going back to Patty's early days. The family lived well. Theirs was a meagre income but the children's needs were always met.

I think this might be a good time to tell you about my next-door neighbour. Please don't think I have lost the plot and beginning to side track into my home life, but you will see that my conversation with Jane Ayres (who is my neighbour) turned out to be a significant act of fate.

It was sometime ago when we met up at the bottom of the garden to have the usual new neighbour yarn. We began to talk about our roots and it transpired that we both had connections to Dulwich in London. One thing led to thirty-three others, when I was amazed to hear that not only did Jane's mother Eileen (same name as my mum) live next door to the Sibley's but she also went out with my Uncle Bill. What a coincidence. Jane kindly arranged a meeting for me with Eileen Tessier, as she is now called, and Jane's sister Anne who also had memories of those early days in Dulwich.

On my first meeting I took some pictures along and Eileen recognised all the family members - and named them. I could not believe my luck. To have someone who had first hand knowledge of the Sibley family from an outsider's point of view was such a stroke of luck. I knew then that the time had come to get this book on the road.

On the second meeting I travelled far (next-door) to again meet up with this most charming lady. I was armed with even more pictures and a tape recorder. The following has been typed up from the taped interview:

"I first met the Sibleys when they lived next door to us at 110 Woodward Road (in Dulwich, South East London) I did not know your mum very well, only that she used to go out with a butcher. I knew Pat well. She was gorgeous. She was fourteen years old when we first met. She was a real character. I never knew their surname, I always called her mother mum, and I knew she was from the East End. Mum ruled the roost, I would hear her shout; "Pat will you get that washing up done." Pat was just Pat, she most certainly was not Anne Shelton. Neither she nor Jo seemed to spend a lot of time at school. Bill, Pat's father, hardly ever spoke, he was really a very quiet gentleman. Then there was Jo, who was such a pretty little girl with the most beautiful black hair. When my mum went up town shopping she would sometimes buy Jo a frock, she was such a dear little girl. I remember how different the two girls were. Jo was like her mother very dark hair and brown eyes and she was very small. Jo was a really good singer and she would tap dance, and was very bubbly. I always thought it was her that was destined to be a star.

Pat was always a big girl for her age, and had lighter hair with blue eyes. They were always having what they called 'rehearsals' we were invited, and the entertainments were held in the Sibley's front room. A show would be put on by the two girls and was always such fun.

We were together the day that war was declared 3rd September 1939. We heard the news on the radio. Seated in our lounge, we watched as the balloons went up from Alleyns College playing field. The noise from the RAF who were occupying the fields was very loud. Eileen was so frightened and upset at the prospect of being bombed, she became very upset. Pat turned to her and said, "Don't worry Eileen, God will look after and protect us.

A story I must tell you. Mum (Mrs Sibley) during the blitz went shopping with my mother to Brixton to buy some furniture. There was not a lot of cash available, but that did not stop your gran. She bought this new bedroom suite and had it delivered to the house. Shortly afterwards the store was bombed to the ground and along with it went all the records of the accounts, so she never did pay for it.

Pat and her family moved away soon after she started with Ambrose. They moved to 142 Court Lane, Dulwich. Pat always told me that one day when she had enough money she would *buy a house in Court Lane, and she did. It was 1940 when she started with Ambrose. Shortly after that I moved back to Brixton to help my father who was a hairdresser to the stars in Brixton High Street, we always had a close contact to the stars in those days.*

I remember her brother Bill with fondness. He was charming, most certainly had the family charm. Sadly that relationship was not to be. Our circumstances were not right so there was no romantic development in our friendship.

The Sibleys were a very interesting family you know. Pat made it all on her own, she had no one behind her to push and promote her, just her and her mum. As I have said she was a wonderful girl. They were all such happy people, always laughing, and a very close family. We sadly lost contact, as a lot of people did during the war years.

Pat was so good looking. I am not surprised she became that gorgeous pin up girl - the Forces Favourite. I always thought her rival, Vera Lynn, was so flat in comparison and there is no doubt Anne had the better voice.

I was saddened to read about her death, very upsetting. She had the most beautiful hands and nails, they were always perfectly painted. Her personality went along with her voice.

Many, many years later, Anne Shelton came to the Congress Theatre Eastbourne, where I was living. I went to see the show, and my family said that I should have gone backstage and asked to see her. I never did as I thought she might not have remembered me. You ask me my lasting memory of her? Well, all I can say is that they were the most marvellous family that I have ever met and I will never forget them.

(This account was given by Mrs Eileen Tessier, who was born on 5/10/1916. Her maiden name was Lauper, and at the time of knowing my family, her name was Lettington.)

~*~

I would very much like to thank Eileen for her colourful account of Patty's early days. It was so fortuitous to have met her through her daughter Jane. The one thing that I did say to Eileen during the afternoon that I spent with her recording her memories, is that she should have gone backstage to see Patty that time in Eastbourne, as she would have certainly remembered her and would have made her most welcome. Patty never forgot anyone that she met and her welcome was always warm.

So, I am now ending the first chapter of this, as Mrs Tossier said, "most marvellous family"of which I am so proud to be a part. I now move on to cover the transformation of a very young Catholic convent girl Patty Sibley to a mega star Anne Shelton....

Chapter Two

The Little Lady From Dulwich

The first record that the young Patty Sibley ever recorded was with Jack Hylton and his Orchestra back in January 1936, entitled *Moanin' Minnie*. At that time Patty was still a convent girl. I am not sure what the nuns would have thought had they known, but regardless she recorded the song under her own name, as she was yet to emerge as Anne Shelton. The song was a somewhat jazzy number and fitted her voice so well. (Incidentally this song is still available on a CD compilation called *Anne Shelton*, released by Evergreen Melodies 01242 537900.)

Bill and Lamma Sibley were very aware of their middle daughter's incredible talent and wanted her to have the chance to show others her gift. It may be of interest to know that Patty never had a singing lesson in her life. Both parents worked long and hard at getting their daughter known to the powers that be in the broadcasting industry. Their hard work and belief in Patty paid off, as she made her first broadcast on a programme put out by the BBC called *Monday Night at Eight*, which featured a spot each week dedicated to promoting new talent, called 'May We Introduce'.

This proved to be a very popular show and a Godsend for many young, up and coming artists such as Patty. The show was produced and presented by a gentleman called Ronnie Waldman, who in those days was a very big name in the BBC hierarchy, someone on the lines of today's X Factor celebrity judge Simon Cowell, one would think.

Patty's father, Bill, had read in the press that the BBC were inviting hopefuls to audition for the 'May We Introduce' spot. It was a very big step but Bill and Lamma truly believed that their daughter had what it took to be a star. They knew that she was destined to be a singer with great potential. Patty's name was put forward and she was granted an audition. There was great excitement in the Sibley household. Patty and Eileen talked about what she should wear, if she should wear makeup (if her mother would let her) and how should she wear her hair, there was so much more to discuss. No doubt there were very many late night discussions between the sisters with a jug of milk and a few homemade biscuits for good measure.

The big day came on 30th May 1940 (the day before Eileen's 24th birthday).

Patty, now known as Anne, went with her mother and sister Eileen to the BBC studios in White Ladies Road, Bristol where they met Ronnie Waldman who was very impressed at the maturity in her voice. He arranged for her to appear in the show. This was the break Patty needed, and it changed her life forever.

Patty was introduced as, "The little lady with a grand smile, Anne Shelton from Dulwich".

She went on to sing *Let The Curtain Come Down*. It was well received and after her performance Ronnie Waldman said to her on air; "I don't know about the curtain coming down on you young lady, I think it's on its way up."

Now one could say this is where fate played a hand in this young lady's future, as listening to the show was one of Britain's top bandleaders, a chap you may well have heard of, namely Bert Ambrose. He was so impressed with what he had heard on 'May We Introduce' that he phoned Ronnie Waldman and said that he wanted to meet this young lady from Dulwich...

At this time Ambrose was looking for a replacement for his current female vocalist Vera Lynn, who was planning to leave. He believed that the young Anne was the very person to replace the much older Vera Lynn.

True to his word Ronnie Waldman phoned Mr and Mrs Sibley

with the invitation from Ambrose. He relayed that they would like Patty to go for another audition, this time with the great bandleader himself!

She attended the audition in June 1940 at the Mayfair Hotel in London's famous West End, as always she was accompanied by her mother. An interesting point to note, Anne never ever, even up to the day she died went anywhere on her own, either to perform, or even shopping.

The young lady from Dulwich was very nervous but also very excited at the prospect of singing with one of the biggest names in the Big Band sounds. Ambrose was very gentle with the young singer, and asked her if she knew the song *Begin the Beguine*? To this she answered, "Yes". He then went on to ask her what key she sang in. The convent girl replied, "I know nothing about keys Mr Ambrose, only that they open doors." This comment was probably an attempt at humour from a nervous young performer. Ambrose's response was a hearty laugh, obviously wanting her to feel relaxed. He suggested they try the song in F Flat, which they did. Ambrose was so impressed that he signed her up immediately to sing with his band as a more than able replacement for Vera Lynn.

For whatever reason, Patty Sibley was not considered an appropriate name for an up and coming star, strange really, as I think it has a ring to it, but it was not to be. So between Bill, Lamma and no doubt the siblings, the name Anne Shelton had been created. Sadly, I have no stories, nor do I have any idea, as to why the name was chosen. I do wish I had asked when younger, as now there is no one left to ask. So we must assume that AS was the approved stage name.

Once signed to Ambrose there was no looking back for Anne. Her debut broadcast with the Ambrose Orchestra was made on the Friday of the same week that she auditioned with them.

By now Anne was well on her way to a new life in the world of show business. The change was only professional, as her newfound fame did not change her home life whatsoever, and it never did.

I remember my mum saying how very hard it was to call Patty 'Anne' in public. It must have been really strange, having to get used to answering to another name but as I have previously mentioned, at home, life had not changed for Pat/Anne. She still had to help with the chores of washing up, housework and all the other household tasks and was still kept in line by her ever strict mother. This kept the young Pat's feet firmly on the ground.

By now World War Two was well under way, having been declared on the 3rd September 1939. It was early 1941 and Anne was continuing with her successful career as the new girl with Ambrose, or Ammy as she had now been encouraged to call him. He always referred to her as Pat...never Anne, unless in public. Most people close to her called her Pat or Patty throughout her life, so as mentioned earlier it seems a shame she decided to discard her own name, don't you think? Patty went on to sign an agreement with Ambrose on 22nd April 1941 in her real name and, stated as an 'enfant', her father signed as a guarantor. I am delighted to say that I still have the agreement, a copy of which is featured in this biography. There are some interesting terms stated and the agreement was signed for a term of five years.

Back in those days there was obviously just as much pressure on stars to be thin as there is today. There was an article that appeared in *Melody Maker* in the early forties written by a chap named Maurice Burman, who was a one-time member of the Ambrose outfit. When he left Ambrose he became an agent and part-time journalist for various music papers. This particular article was written about Anne and her weight. As she was quite a big girl, Ambrose wanted her to have a course of injections to help her to loose a few pounds. She attended a Harley Street doctor and had a couple of injections but she became most unwell, her mother intervened and refused for Anne to finish the course, stating that she was to remain as God had intended her to be. Good for my Nan I say, believe me no-one in their right mind would have argued with her!

Wireless programmes had been seriously curtailed at the beginning of the war and most live theatres had been closed down in fear of air raid attacks or other unexplained atrocities of war. Listeners to the wireless were only able to hear news bulletins, current affairs programmes, or light music by courtesy of Sandy McPherson's organ recitals and orchestral concerts.

In these dark and gloomy days, with the causalities of war and families losing their loved ones, it was soon realised that some livelier and more light-hearted entertainment was needed to boost the morale and raise the spirits of this strong nation. So in its wisdom, the BBC decide to provide two separate programmes. One was called *The Home Service,* which was mostly used for news bulletins to keep the public up to date with Adolph's latest antics, and it was also a programme featuring classical music. The second choice of listening was *The Light Programme.* The content and music of this programme was not so serious. Eventually a third station was created under the heading of *The Forces Programme.*

As time went by it became evident that the dreaded air raids that were expected at the outbreak of war were not going to happen, well not yet anyway, and there seemed no immediate threat of the promised invasion by the Germans. All the theatres and cinemas started to re-open for 'business as usual' and Anne found herself in great demand. What a truly resilient nation we were, and thankfully still are.

Anne was not only broadcasting with the great Ambrose and his Orchestra, but was also recording with them. As previously mentioned, her first recording for public release was *Begin the Beguine.* This was an immediate success pocketing many sales for her new employer and mentor. Eighteen days later she recorded with equal success *A Nightingale Sang in Berkley Square.*

The record label on which her name first appeared was Decca; it read *'Bert Ambrose and his Orchestra, with vocal refrain by Anne Shelton'.* Although the young Anne was under contract to Ambrose and already recording on the Decca label, Decca were quick to see her great potential and wanted to sign her up to make recordings under her own name, so the label would read; *'Anne Shelton with the Ambrose Orchestra',* in theory she took top billing. Six weeks after recording *Berkley Square*, she recorded *Fools Rush In.*

Anne was allowed to sign a further contract in 1942 with Rex Records, which was a subsidiary of the Decca Recording Company, and the very sought after Anne began recording in her own right. She was still very much under the direction of Ambrose. At this time a very close bond had developed between the two and Ammy was most protective of his young protégé Patty, the girl he had made a star from a young unknown.

There were occasions when Anne recorded the same song on both labels, with different orchestral arrangements. These included *A Pair of Silver Wings* and *Silver Wings in the Moonlight.* Among those accompanying her on these recordings were Billy Ternet and Jay Wilburg, two well-known performers of the time. In those days had there been a 'Top Ten' there is no doubt the name of Anne Shelton would have appeared week after week, featuring songs like, *Coming in on a Wing and a Prayer*, *A Nightingale Sang in Berkley Square*, *My Yiddishe Momma* and *Fools Rush In,* to mention but a few. The sales from these recordings in today's market would have made them all chart entries.

In the 40s such recordings were sold in large chain stores, such as *Woolworths*. The sheet music for songs was also on sale as families often had a piano at home for family entertainment. The sheet music usually had a picture of the artist on the front and would be displayed in the store whilst the particular song was being played. A clever sales pitch, as often this would make a sale of both record and sheet music.

Anne Shelton was now firmly established in show business. In no time at all her popularity grew and grew with the British public. She had won their hearts with her warm, golden voice that carried a note of such sincerity. Anne was constantly on the wireless (as it was called) and she was making more and more recordings.

It was not long before Anne began entertaining the active servicemen at military bases all over the country. With Anne's youthful, pretty appearance, her blonde hair and blue eyes; it was not long before she became the boys' pin-up girl, gaining her recognition as 'Forces Favourite'. The much older artist Vera Lynn was already acclaimed as the Forces Favourite, but Anne was chasing at her heels in popularity.

Life had now changed for the Sibleys, as it had for so many wartime families. Bill the eldest son was in the army serving abroad, and Eileen was still working with George at the butcher shop in Camberwell. George was never called up to enlist, as it was considered that in his role as a butcher it was necessary for him to stay in business and supply what little meat there was (as it was rationed) to the public. Josie, who was still too young to work, was mostly at home. Lamma was Anne's chaperone and their dad, Bill senior, was still maintaining the stability of the family and still working in central London.

Anne had a very heavy schedule. As well as broadcasting and recording, she began touring with Ambrose to the various variety theatres and music halls, which were in abundance during the war years, sadly none to be found today. As mentioned, Anne's mum was her constant companion, leaving Jo in the care of her elder sister and her dad.

It was obvious that Anne had become a great asset to Ambrose. She had an amazing vocal range enabling her to sing Jazz, sentimental, and up-tempo songs. She could hold a note for as long as needed and was the girl of the moment.

The war was progressing; sadly there was no sign of an early end to the conflict. Things started to change. The quiet life that had been enjoyed by most small towns and Home Counties was being replaced by air raids both by day and night, which was becoming a way of life.

Due to the constant bombing in London, a great deal of broadcasting was done from Bristol. This meant even more travelling for artists like Anne and the bands. It must have been very tiring. They were all so devoted to entertaining and doing their bit for the war, that they took it all in their stride.

During such broadcasts it was common that they would suddenly go off air. This usually happened when an air raid was imminent. They went off air to prevent any possibility of enemy aircraft picking up radio signals, which might have assisted them in finding their target easier than perhaps they would have done.

Anne was featured in a new radio show called *Calling Malta* she appeared with a comedian called Ronald Shiner, who was born 8.6.1903. He was a very popular funny chap, who told the story that he was a former Canadian Mountie! I cannot confirm if this is true, but it made interesting reading. He made his stage debut in 1928. Another interesting note about Mr Shiner, is that he once insured his rather large nose with Lloyds for $30,000. The show was very popular and successful as this was the only radio link between the besieged Malta and Great Britain. The inhabitants of Malta were so pleased to have this link, as were the many British with family in Malta.

Calling Malta was launched in 1941 and carried on almost to the end of the war, attracting million of listeners over the years. Surprisingly the show did not have a signature tune, as did most shows at that time. It always began in the same way, Anne would blow a whistle and say 'It's Anne calling Malta'. Most sensational for the day, don't you think? Anne sang live on these shows and featured songs that were current, such as *Kiss The Boys Goodbye*, and other morale boosting numbers.

Anne told a story that was most amusing. One evening just before the show was due to go live, she needed to pay a visit to the 'little girl's room'. Unfortunately the door lock jammed and she was unable to get out. This caused her to panic somewhat, firstly because she was due on air imminently, and secondly she was very claustrophobic....she started to shout for help, trying to hide the panic in her voice, but alas no one came to the damsel's rescue. Anne decided that the only way out of her dilemma was to stand on the loo and climb over the partition to the next cubicle. This she did, and in true professional style she was in time for her 'whistle blowing'. The only tell tail signs were the black marks on her formerly spotless white dress caused by climbing over the partition into the next loo. No one was aware of her unfortunate mishap.

Anne was now enjoying her newfound status and was in a financial position to move onwards and upwards. She wanted to move the family into a larger house, but she was most adamant that she wanted to stay in her beloved Dulwich. A house came onto the market that she was very interested in.

It was once the original farmhouse of Dulwich Village situated overlooking Dulwich Park (a favourite haunt of Queen Victoria, well known for its rhododendrons). I often wonder if at one time Dulwich Park would have been part of the acreage of the original farmland. The house was much larger and older than any other in the lane, and in fact the house took up two houses, as theirs was numbered 142, and then it went to 146, so in fact 142 was also 144 if you see what I mean!

The family moved in to their new home just before Christmas. From a young age Patty Sibley had said that one day she would live in a house in Court Lane and she most certainly did.

Bill Jnr was still overseas fighting in Europe. The remainder of the family Bill Snr, Lamma, Anne (Patty), Eileen and Josie moved into the rather large, six bed roomed farmhouse, which they named Glendower. Anne paid the sum of £5000 for this property; it is hard to believe that now it is worth well over a million. The house was very secluded and hidden from the road. There were gates at either end of a sweeping, circular drive. Two oak pillars supported the porch, standing proud either side of the solid oak front door.

Once inside it was rather like going back in time. As you went through the front door and into the hall, to the right there was the downstairs cloakroom with toilet, wash basin and a huge built in cupboard where all the coats, hats and wellington boots were stored. To the left there was the staircase (the house had three floors), which again had oak panelling. The stairs were very steep and winding to the top of the house. Also on the ground floor, off from the hall there were three doors leading to the lounge, dining room and breakfast room/kitchen.

The lounge was large, with French windows leading into the conservatory. The lounge had an Italian marble surround fireplace. The dining room was oak panelled with exposed beams in the ceiling and a red slate surround open fire. There was a door leading into the conservatory.

A third door led to the breakfast room, which was, as in most families, the most used room. There was a box above the breakfast room door with numbered lights, which were actually bells. Every room in the house had a bell on the wall for the family to press should they need attendance from one of the servants. This was in days gone by...I cannot remember them ever being used by our family, except by me as a child being naughty.

The kitchen was massive with a grey slate floor; there was also a walk in larder, large fridge, which had been imported from the USA, and a double Aga that was the method for cooking.

On the second floor there were six good-sized bedrooms, two at the front of the house, and four at the back. On the third floor there was the billiard room, as it was called. This housed a full sized billiard table and was kitted out better than any club billiard room. Many an evening the room was used for a fun night, they would play billiards; listen to music and have a family night. There was a lovely view from this room, as it was high, and over looked the park. In the distance you could see Crystal Palace Tower and Dulwich and Sydenham Golf Club.

In the grounds on the main lawn there was a beautiful Weeping Willow. The courtyard at the back of the house was covered with a very healthy Wisteria, (this was Patty's pride and joy, and became her responsibility to keep in check! She kept this task until she moved out of Court Lane in 1994). There was a tennis court and vegetable garden. This was a truly beautiful property, which soon became home to the family and remained so for the next fifty years.

Despite all the work that no doubt was needed on the new home, it was left to Bill senior, Jo and Eileen to attend to, as 'Anne' was once again on the road entertaining.

In 1942 Anne was given her first 'very own' show, entitled *'Introducing Anne'*, which was to be beamed to our troops in North Africa with the intention to counteract Nazi propaganda in the African desert. This was such a great honour for Anne, as it was the Prime Minister of the day, Winston Churchill, who suggested she should be used for the programme, "because of the warmth and sincerity in her voice and her popularity with the troops".

The Germans of course had their own Forces Favourite. Her name was Lale Anderson, she sang a song, which originated from Germany, called *Lilli Marlene*, this was frequently featured in the propaganda broadcast referred to. The programme was picked up on the airwaves by British troops in the desert as well as the Germans. This was thought to be a bad idea for our boys, who did not understand the German lyrics, but did like the tune. The British authorities decided to have the lyrics written in English but they would have to be modified, as a simple translation of this song, would not have been fitting for the young Anne to sing, as *Lilli Marlene* was about a prostitute, (How protective we were then of our young performers, I wondered if such thought would be given now?) The chosen one to write the new lyric was Tommy Connor, who was a well-known songwriter at the time. Anne not only recorded this new *Lilli Marlene*, but also had it as her signature tune for her new show. Until the new lyrics had been written, Anne's voice was still beamed to Africa, but she had to 'la la' the song, which she really hated.

The recording was a huge success for her and a really big seller. It has been said that Anne's version also became a hit with the German troops.

The '*Introducing Anne*' show was so popular that they decided to give her a further series, surprisingly called '*Introducing Anne Again*'. The signature tune for this show was not, as everyone expected *Lilli Marlene,* but in fact it was *With a Smile and a Song*. The tune was used for most, if not all of Anne's future broadcasts and appearances in variety, which is why I felt it was a fitting name for her biography.

As many of you may already know, *With a Smile and a Song* is from the Walt Disney cartoon Snow White. Disney and Anne met when she was in America, and he presented her with a signed framed picture of *Snow White and the Seven Dwarfs,* which I still have today.

Anne was now well established in the business and making close friends with many well-known artists of the day. One of the people who became a life long friend, as well as her musical director and pianist was Stanley Black, who with his orchestra accompanied her on all her BBC productions and other shows and broadcasts.

There seemed no end to her talents. Before long Anne was branching out from singing, turning her attention to acting. Still in the 1940's Anne appeared in three films, *King Arthur was a Gentleman, Bees in Paradise* and *Miss London Ltd.* Her sister Jo made brief appearances in two of these films. She starred alongside Arthur Askey, Evelyn Dall, Max Bacon, Jack Train, Jean Kent and various other names. There was a fourth film called *Come Dance with Me* in which she shared the starring role with Derek Roy, Max Wall and Anton Karas (who was known as the Zither man). Sadly this is the only film that I do not have a copy of, and I have never seen. I would very much like to see it, so if anyone has a copy please let me know.

Although Anne's acting career never overtook her singing, the films were greatly enjoyed by her fans, but they never exactly broke box office records.

The pretty little convent girl from Dulwich was growing up to become a most attractive young woman who was the pin up girl of many young men, especially those overseas in the Forces. She was well on her way to being the Forces Favourite.

I am sure most of you reading this will be aware that on 6th June 1944 the Allied Forces began the D-Day operations by invading and landing on the Normandy beaches. Shortly after the invasion the Germans began reprisals on England, bombing us with the V1 bomber also known as the 'Doodlebug'. These bombs were different to the conventional bombs, as they made the most ear-piercing noise when approaching. A sound resembling hundreds of motor bike engines roaring all at once, is how it was described to me, then suddenly the engine would cut out, leaving the missile to dive straight down, landing on houses, shops, offices, schools, hospitals in fact any building in its path. These bombs caused much havoc and loss of life in London and the Home Counties.

My aunt told me a story about when she was appearing at the Finsbury Park Empire in North London. She was about half way through her act, and as usual she was singing to a full house. Suddenly a Doodlebug could be heard approaching it was so close, that the noise was drowning out the singer and the orchestra. Then came the awaited silence as the engine cut out. They all knew their fate would be decided in the next few seconds, would they be saved, or was their number up? My aunt said the seconds they waited seemed like hours and that her heart was beating so fast it was like drumming in her ears. She whispered; "Please dear God, save us", then came the loud explosion as the missile dropped further along the road, much to the relief of those at the theatre.

When things quietened down a member of the audience shouted out, "best start that song again Anne, we did not hear the best part with all that bloody noise going on." Such was the mood, and uplifting spirits of the majority of the public. They were so fed up at having their lives turned upside down in one way or another and determined not to be broken by the constant bombardment. That night, Anne said that she thought the Doodlebugs were following her around, as one had fallen very close to her Dulwich home.

Anne carried on through the year, playing at theatres all over London, dodging the Doodlebugs and boosting the morale of her fellow Londoners. Later in 1944 the Germans introduced their other secret weapon called the V2. This was a rocket, loaded with tons of high explosives. Unlike the V1 there was no audible sign of their approach. The rockets were fired across the channel very frequently, day and night. The neverending bombing by the Germans was intended to shatter the heart and soul of the inhabitants of this great country, but thankfully this did not happen.

The entertainers of those days were real troopers. They took all the heartbreak, sadness and devastation in their stride and kept a smile on their face, a song in their heart, and remembered the show must go on. They helped to keep the nation going strong and provided a little light relief in such harrowing times. For this, those celebrity 'troopers' of the war years will always be remembered with fondness and gratitude for many years to come.

Chapter Three

Anne, Glenn and Bing.....

Due to the impending D-Day operations England became host to thousands upon thousands of American and Canadian soldiers, sailors and airmen. All were here in preparation for the planned invasion of occupied France and other German occupied countries. The allied troops were mostly young men far away from home. They wanted, in fact needed, entertaining during their off duty hours. As were all overseas service personnel, they were missing home and their way of life in their own countries, they wanted something to remind them of home life before the war.

At that time there was a great American bandleader who was well aware of the young servicemen's needs, that was Glenn Miller, or Captain Glenn Miller to give him his correct title at the time. Glenn had an idea. He wanted to come to England to entertain the American troops, but not on his own, he wanted to bring his original band with him. All the guys in his band were serving in the US forces, but were not all stationed together. His plan was to re-unite them all, come to England and entertain the boys. Under his command the group was formed and he was given permission to carry out his idea. So Glenn Miller arrived in England with his band, his own singers and a complete working group as he had had in America.

Glenn had to work closely with the BBC, as they were the only corporation able to broadcast the shows. It was not long before Glenn became aware of the young English singer Anne Shelton. He heard her sing and felt that her voice suited his sound. He wanted her to sing with his band and it would appear what

Captain Miller wanted, Captain Miller got!

Ambrose was approached and asked if Anne would be able to appear on several of Glenn's broadcasts, this he gave consideration to, surely he would not have denied the young star such an opening? It so happened that the BBC VIPs, had already been having meetings to discuss the format of possible shows with Glenn, not only for Anne, but also for other popular British artists such as Denny Dennis, Gloria Brent, Beryl Davies, Paula Green, Sam Browne and many more. It happened that Anne made several appearances with Miller, both in broadcasts and concerts for the troops.

When Anne first met Glenn Miller, she herself said she was a "chopsy little madam" She put it down to the "arrogance of youth". Here is her account of their first meeting:

"I remember walking onto the stage looking like a pre-war bag of flour, as I was white with fear. Captain Miller greeted me and said, 'here is the little girl who sings in G flat.' I said, 'how do you do Captain Miller. Yes, I believe I do sing in G flat. Are you able to play in G flat as Mr Ambrose can?'"

Anne also mentioned how she had cringed in later years to think that she had asked Glenn if his pianist had to be so 'busy' on the piano. Anne often recalled this memory and said how, in later years, she was embarrassed to think of her upfront attitude to such a great star. The song that Anne first sang with Glenn was *I'll Get By*.

Glenn Miller's live concerts first began in London but soon moved across to Bedfordshire due to the bombardment by the Germans. It was reported that Glenn was not keen to stay in London under such threatening circumstances. In fairness the orchestra did in fact have a narrow escape when the building in which they had been billeted was practically demolished after a flying bomb had dropped outside behind a parked army truck. Fortunately the band was not in the building at the time. It was sometimes necessary for the band to return to London for recording commitments in the studio, but they were most reluctant to stay any longer than need be.

This meant that Anne and other stars appearing with Glenn had to make many journeys from London and back, often in the same day. Such was the pace of life in wartime London and indeed many other places in the country.

As mentioned previously, Anne went on to appear several times with Glenn and they formed a fond friendship. Towards the end of their professional relationship, which sadly ended with Glenn's disappearance and assumed death, he gave her a gold bracelet and told her "there is more gold in your voice, than there is in the bracelet". Anne kept the bracelet all her life.

Anne was asked by Glenn to accompany him on the flight to Versailles for the Christmas show (15.12.1944) as we all know, that was the doomed flight that never arrived. Glenn and his fellow passengers have never been found. Had Anne been allowed to go with him, we would have lost two great talents that day instead of one.

There were two reasons why Anne did not travel to France with Glenn. Firstly Ambrose (who was somewhat jealous of the professional relationship that had blossomed between Anne and Glenn) would not release her from her contract to appear in six *Workers Playtimes*, and secondly, Anne would not have been happy to travel without her mother, or to be away from her home and family at Christmas time.

At their last meeting before he left England, Glenn told Anne that when the war was over, she should go Stateside and work with him in the United States. Although Anne did go to the USA in the 50s and was a great success, sadly it was not with Glenn Miller. As a point of interest Anne Shelton was the last British singer to broadcast with Glenn Miller and his band, as thereafter Glenn dispensed with guest singers and used his own vocalists.

~*~

Anne it appeared was not only appreciated by her own countrymen but was also a hit with the Americans over here. The same year 1944, another great American star came over to England to entertain the troops as Miller had done - Bing Crosby. Crosby heard Anne, and by now her most distinctive voice and he also requested to have Anne sing with him. Miss Shelton was in great demand.

Anne and Bing appeared together on the BBC's weekly radio show 'Variety Bandbox'. After an amusing banter between the two, they sang two duets *Easter Parade* and a song Anne was well associated with, *I'll Get By*. After the duets, there was rapturous applause. Anne and Bing went on to entertain more troops, about four thousand in all, with an impromptu concert at the Mayfair Club in London. *(This duet of Anne and Bing is also featured on the CD *Thank You Captain Miller*)

My aunt recalled the very first time she met Bing. A most amusing story that I would like to relay to you now. Anne was broadcasting her own show '*Anne to You*' the show was live and coming from the Monseigneur restaurant in Jermyn Street, London. About half an hour before she went on air she received a telephone call asking her to go to the Queensbury Club (The London Casino), as Bing Crosby was there, he wanted to meet her and for her to sing with him. The young Anne thought it had to be a practical joke and did not take the call at all seriously, in fact she flippantly replied to the caller; "Sorry, I cannot come to meet Mr Crosby as I am having tea with the King."

Anne did not give the mystery call another thought but about ten minutes later she had another call, this time she recognised the voice to be Cecil Madden, who was a well known BBC producer of the time. He confirmed that it was not a hoax and that Bing did want her to appear with him at the Mayfair Club, and asked her to go to Mayfair immediately after her broadcast. Anne was still not 100% convinced it was for real. Her sister Eileen (my mum) was with her and said, "it can't be a joke we had better go". Anne phoned her mother and told her to send the car to the Mayfair Club to collect her later, as she had been invited to sing with Mr Crosby. Her mother was so excited, as was Anne, but she was also nervous.

After the broadcast Anne and Eileen jumped into a taxi and headed for the club. They arrived at the stage door and went down to the back stage, which appeared to be empty. Anne turned to her sister and said, "told you it was a joke". Then from nowhere an American officer appeared and asked Anne if she was indeed Anne Shelton and said that he had been looking for her. He escorted her to a dressing room, upon opening the door Anne saw sitting at his dressing table the man himself....Bing Crosby. He said to her "Hi Anne my gal, I am glad you came and have agreed to sing with me." For Anne, she recalled, it was a dream. He put his arm around her and asked if she was ok. She told him she thought she was going to faint....but as always kept her cool. So this was their first meeting. The appearance of the two on stage was electric.

Anne and Bing became firm friends over the coming years and it was a friendship that lasted up until Bing's death.

~*~

Variety Band Box went on broadcasting for many years after the war. The venue for the broadcast moved from Queensbury All Services Club to the Camberwell Palace in South East London, this was nearer to Anne's home in Dulwich. Later on the venue changed again to the People's Palace in Mile End Road, East London. Anne continued to be a frequent guest artist. Eventually, several years later, the Queensbury Club was re-named The London Casino.

The war seemed to be going on forever. Anne was wise and older than her years in maturity. I am sure that during those years the young had to grow up fast and did not have the luxury of the carefree years of youth that many of us born after the war enjoyed.

Apart from her constant appearances in shows for the forces and general public, a much more caring and serious side of Anne's career was emerging. She made frequent visits to the wounded in Military hospitals and nursing homes. One such visit that she told me of was to the Guinea Pig unit in East Grinstead, West Sussex. This unit was where airmen and other military personnel were taken having sustained serious burns whilst on active service. The injuries often caused horrific disfiguration. These badly burnt lads were mostly under the expert care of the renowned surgeon Archibald Macindoe, who later received a Knighthood for the pioneering work that he had done.

On one visit to the hospital after touring the wards, the young lieutenant who was assigned to accompany Anne asked if she would be prepared to do an impromptu show for some of the lads on the ward who had the most horrendous injuries and were very badly disfigured. Anne at once said that she would. Her pianist for the show was a young airman who was delighted at the opportunity to play for her. The patients were in a darkened room awaiting the arrival of their pin up girl 'Anne Shelton' Before Anne entered the room, the young lieutenant who prompted this show said to her that they would keep the lights very low, as she might find the sight of these men's injuries too upsetting. Anne's response was very clear. She said, "There is no need to dim the lights; I want to see the boys that I am singing to". This she did, not only did she sing, she walked amongst them, talked and joked with them and gave several a kiss on the cheek.

Her heart must have been in her boots. She told me she felt so upset to see the poor lads with such horrific injuries. Some had virtually no face at all, no eyelids, lips or ears. Much of their skin had been grafted from other parts of their body to try and repair their faces. I think my aunt was very brave to do what she did, bearing in mind how young she was. It most certainly was a memory that stayed with her for life. She was always so thankful for what the service personnel did for us in the war and often reminded me when I was younger, "If it was not for the bravery of those young lads and lasses you would not be here today". This I do know and I will always be thankful, and will never forget what the forces did, in fact still do, to keep this country as it should be - free.

The East Grinstead burns unit went on to do some absolutely

marvellous work performing so many pioneering operations. After the war the Guinea Pig Club was formed and I do believe it is still going.

It was in this year that Anne met her future husband David Reid. David was a Lieutenant aboard H.M.S Tormentor. They met on 5th December 1944.

Anne was travelling down to do a show for the crew of the Tormentor and David was sent as the 'entertainments officer' to accompany Anne to Portsmouth. They hit it off at once. David was a good-looking, dark haired Scot. The young Anne fell in love with him at first glance. One would be forgiven to think that a young attractive star like Anne would have had many boyfriends but she did not, always being accompanied by her mum, and I imagine would-be suitors were kept at a distance. David was obviously the 'only' one that was to be allowed to enter into the Shelton world.

They started courting shortly after that first meeting, needless to say, their romance was conducted under the very strict, Catholic eye of Mrs Sibley! My aunt told me how embarrassed she felt the first time she waved David goodbye at Portsmouth Railway Station. Anne was returning to London after the show on the Tormentor, on their parting she said that she did the corniest little wave, with her hand close to her face, head tilted and eyes wide opened. In later years she would joke with me saying, "Well if that didn't put your Uncle David off, nothing would!"

The relationship was slow to blossom, and their meetings were few and far between. David was Anne's first boyfriend and intimate moments were most certainly not often! He moved into the family home in 1945 after the War, and his leaving the Navy. They had separate rooms for many years and, like the good Catholic girl that she was, it stayed that way for many years.

It is lovely to think that their relationship lasted as long as it did. They were faithful to each other, as theirs was a true love, a bit like those in a Barbara Cartland novel. Anne and David stayed together until his death in 1990. They had their ups and downs, but don't we all?

We are now back to 1945, May 8th which signalled the end of the European War. Those that survived thanked God in no small way I am sure. Gradually the men and women in the three services came home. As did the school children who had been evacuated to the countryside of England. Before long a new, most welcome, almost forgotten lifestyle resumed. What delight there must have been for the parents to welcome home their sons and daughters, and for girlfriends and boyfriends to be reunited after so long. Happily England was returning to normality.

Some now were describing Anne as being England's most popular female singer. Her schedule was very busy. One of her commitments was an appearance in a BBC programme called 'The Ambrose Cavalcade'. Other stars appearing in the show were Elsie Carlisle, Sam Brown, Max Bacon, Evelyn Dall, Jack Cooper and Vera Lynn, all former members and performers with his orchestra. Ambrose only ever had the crème de la crème of show business work for him, to appear with his band was the greatest accolade one could achieve. It was a superb cast that gave an overwhelming show.

The Sibley family (now more often known as Shelton) were still very much together. My Granddad did not take kindly to the discarding of his family name, as he was very old fashioned and wanted very much to stay in the background, in total contrast to my Nan, who loved to be called Shelton, and was enjoying the shine and the glory of fame. She revelled in being the mother to a number one star, and was the driving force behind Anne.

By this time my mum Eileen had married her sweetheart George Richards, and they had a baby called Stephanie (my sister) who was affectionately called Didda (Irish for darling) by my mum's family. This nickname was not recognised by my dad's relatives, as sadly there was no love loss between the two families. The Richards, (that is to say mainly my father's mother) had a very low opinion of those in show business. I never met my paternal Nan, Alice, as she died the day I was born, guess it must have been the shock of a new arrival! I gather she was not an easy woman to be around, and she had an overpowering control over my dad and his three brothers. Back to the biography, Jo was blossoming into a truly beautiful woman with her very Latin looks, so different to her sisters who were both blonde. Bill was back from the war and working for Anne, mostly as her chauffeur. I think it was fair to say that Anne, although her father was still working, was the main bread-winner supporting the whole family one way or another, with the exception of my parents.

The conflict with Japan carried on until August 1945, from then onwards England was finally at peace with the world.

~*~

1946 saw Anne with another new weekly radio series entitled *With a Smile and a Song* (what a good name!) on the BBC light programme. She was accompanied on the piano once again by her friend Stanley Black along with BBC variety orchestra. The programme commenced on 18th December 1946, until 22nd January 1947. The show was very similar in format to the previous series. One of the features was to invite amateur songwriters to submit their songs to the BBC and, if they were good enough to be chosen, Anne would sing the song on a future show.

As time went on Anne made more and more broadcasts with shows like *Music Hall, Henry Hall's Guest Night, Workers Playtime* and *Variety Fanfare.* Anne was well received always giving her all. She had a vast following with her now most distinct sound, not only in this country but also in the USA.

In 1947 she was invited to appear in America, an invitation that she accepted, accompanied as usual by her mother, fiancé David and her pianist. Anne made a great impression on the Americans and was a great success. Other British stars to travel and perform in the States at that time were Beryl Davis and George Shearing.

Going back to the variety tours in England during the 40s, they must have been very exhausting for the entertainers, as often stars would be appearing at more than one venue on the same day. This required them to dash into a waiting car after one performance, to arrive at the next venue just in time for their second appearance of the evening. It is very fortunate that back in those days the volume of traffic and the hold ups, were not as we know them now.

Anne was usually billed on the programme as "The Golden Voice of Radio" and after her successful tour of the States she was billed "The Golden Voice of Two Continents" A typical show featuring Anne would include her singing a selection of songs such as *Blue Skies, The Old Lamplighter, The Postman Passes Me By, Among My Souvenirs, A Gal In Calico, A Rainy Night In Rio, Spring Will Be A Little Late This Year* and *Tenement Symphony* to name but a few. There was always a spot in her show where she would walk away from the microphone (which in those days were permanent fixtures to the stage) and she would stand by the piano on stage and sing without the mike. This would usually be *The Bells Of St Mary's* or *Now Is The Hour.* I think she did this to prove to the audience how very strong her voice was and that she did not really need a microphone to deliver her song.

Anne's first pianist when she went solo was Frank Still. He was a brilliant accompanist. Anne always encouraged a little jovial banter between the two of them between numbers, which was much appreciated by the audience. This was something that Anne went on to do with all her pianists, even up until her last show in 1994. She had the most amazing sense of humour with a very quick wit. She would have made a very good comedienne.

Anne's working relationship ended with Frank Still when he left England to go to America where he married a well-known American film star called Martha Raye. His place was filled by another well-known musician, Johnnie Spence. Anne was very fond of Johnnie, and he became a close friend and visitor to the family home in Court Lane. Johnnie remained Anne's pianist and musical director for many years until he left to form his own orchestra and went on to become a record producer with Top Rank records. Anne hated variation in routine and felt very vulnerable when she had to change pianists, which is something she did many times during her career.

1948 was the period known as The Cold War, so named because of the tension between the Soviet Union and the Western Allies. This conflict resulted in a blockade of Berlin, whereby the city was divided into two sections, East and West Germany. The Eastern half was ruled by the Soviet authorities and the Western half by the Allies. Everything essential to every day living became very scarce to those in both sectors. Due to this most unsatisfactory situation an operation named 'The Berlin Airlift' was launched, this involved England transporting by plane essential food and other needed supplies to the people of Germany affected by this situation to try and make their day-to-day lives a little easier.

Although the war finished in 1945, many of our troops were still stationed there, so it was decided to put on some entertainment for the lads. The entertainment was planned to be in the form of a musical show. The troops were asked which artist they would like to entertain them, due to space on the aircraft they could only have one artist, without any hesitation, or debate they chose Anne Shelton. My aunt told of how she was piled on the plane bound for Germany along with sacks of coal, mail and other essentials. Whilst she was there she did twelve concerts for the troops in three days. One of these concerts was transmitted to the BBC Light Programme, and ironically, the concert chosen to be transmitted was relayed from what had been Hitler's own theatre, which had survived the allied bombing raids. I remember how very proud my aunt felt, and how emotional it was for her to sing *My Yiddishe Momma* from Hitler's stage, considering he had been responsible for the persecution and death of so many Jews, and now this song, for the first time since long before the war, was being sung with such feeling from a German stage. She chose to sing it as a tribute to all the Jews who had died, and for those still remaining who had experienced such an awful ordeal.

My aunt had many close friends that were Jewish, and it was thought by many that in fact she was also a Jewess. This was understandable as Anne gave such an incredible deliverance of songs such as *Yiddishe Momma*, and *Eli Eli*, both were so closely linked to the Jewish community. But, as I am sure most of you know she was a very devout Roman Catholic. There are great similarities between the two faiths, insofar as family means everything, and the mother is the head figure of the family. This was very much the case with Anne.

Anne had now begun recording on the Decca and Rex labels but soon after this moved over to HMV. On this label she recorded with Geoff Love, Ken Mackintosh, Frank Cordell, George Melachrino, and Reg Owen. This move now takes us into the fifties... and another chapter.

Chapter Four

The Fabulous 50s

The Fifties was a decade that was to be the zenith of Anne's career. She became even busier with radio broadcasts, recording dates and variety tours.

In 1951 Anne made her second visit to the USA. The tour was planned to last for three months but, as Glenn Miller had predicted, her popularity was such in the States that her tour lasted for almost a year. It could have been extended even further but, as it was approaching Christmas, Anne wanted to go home. Throughout her career she was never away from home at Christmas time, as this was always a time to be with family as far as she was concerned.

During her tour Anne made appearances and broadcasts from coast to coast. She also took part in a hook up feature with *Two Way Family Favourites* which was a regular spot on the BBC Light Programme every Sunday lunch time. During the show requests were played between the USA and England. The host for the show here was Franklin Englemann and the American host was a well-known disc jockey called Skitch Henderson.

This programme became a great success, as by this time there were many English girls who had married American servicemen that had been stationed in England, and had now returned to the States, many with their new brides. In this particular programme Anne was exchanging messages and wisecracking with Franklin, he also played some of her recordings. Franklin Englemann was a great admirer of Anne and used her wartime recording of *I'll be Seeing You* as a signature tune for one of his own weekly BBC programmes.

Anne was really enjoying the popularity in the US and was getting on well with the Americans with whom she was coming into close contact. I remember her telling me about her meeting with some Italian gentlemen who were now resident in America. She said how very important they were and how they offered to have her work full-time for them in the many clubs that they owned in New York. This offer was declined most graciously by her mother, and it is just as well, as Anne later found out that the very wealthy, somewhat overpowering 'gentlemen' that she had encountered had been part of the Mafia! Anne had to have it explained to her, as she had no idea what the Mafia was. When she was told she said, "what a shame, they seemed such nice Catholic boys."

Anne was the first British female singer to appear at the world famous Copacabana Club in New York. She played there for a month, also touring to Las Vegas, San Francisco, Hollywood, Chicago, Washington and Philadelphia. She met many stars including Bob Hope, Frankie Lane, Sophie Tucker, Judy Garland, Sammy Davis Jnr and Johnnie Ray, who absolutely adored her, and she was very fond of him. They stayed close friends right up until his death on 24th February 1990.

Here follows two extracts from 'Variety' and 'Billboard' regarding Anne's performances at the Copacabana

Extract from *Variety* - August 15th 1951 Copacabana, New York.

'Anne Shelton is perhaps the most famed pop singer from England, thanks to her London recordings and an inherent vocal appeal. She's not in the Gracie Fields idiom as a British stylist - she's a latter day disc product, akin to the many thrushes who enjoy the sudden upsurge to fame and fortune, thanks to the magic of the Platters. (This is on the plus side of the current hassle and the disc jockey's potency and prestige in disproportion to true values, but that's another discussion. And for more of which see the Music Dept)

Miss Shelton must experience comparison to Kate Smith,

Sophie Tucker, Belle Baker, for two reasons; her vocal appeal and her somewhat generous proportions. She has the softness of Miss Smith, the appeal of Miss Baker in her vaudeville heyday, and can get low down with *Some of These Days* which she actually renders in the Tucker tradition. That's a pretty good parlay to begin with, if only for comparisons, but it should be added that Miss Shelton's own intrinsic values would catapult her to American attention even without this triple threat comparative standard.

She certainly knows how to use the mike, and in her occasional discursions away from the mike she manifests a full range voice that could fill even as tough a room as the Copa.

Her buxom personality is draped in an attractive black lace-over-green gown and both set off her strawberry blonde good looks. In turn, her vocal prowess is the convincer. She makes her half hour on the floor a tour-de-force as she unreels songs such as *Shanghai*, *Too Young*, *Beguine*, *Mr Mississippi*, *Some of These Days*, a novelty *Tippery Samba* and *Yiddishe Momma* the last two genuine encores. The Irish novelty is different and while some of the regulars mildly gasp at the thought of *Yiddishe Momma* once again, Miss Shelton has the wisdom to sing it only in its English Lyrical version. And in her manner of presentation it would also click with the Texas trade at Houston's Shamrock Hotel.

English songstress evidences authority and warmth. She handles some of her introductory spiels about Anglo-U.S. song exchanges with intelligence, mentioning the BBC discs and Allied troops entertainment in a matter-of-fact but impressive manner, yet not over-stressing.

It is only in her well chosen, between songs dialogue that a slight British accent asserts itself. Her pop lyrics are seemingly purposely phrased for the American ear, and with American diction, which is an apparent schooling because of her London records disc-ing which have been strongly primed for the American market. The local home grown English record buyers traditionally like the Yank inflection even more than our sympaticao for a pleasant British brogue.

This is Miss Shelton's Yank in person debut and judging by her Copa click she can take out citizenship papers right now'

Extract from *Billboard* - **August 18th 1951   Copacabana, New York**

'Anne Shelton's preem was anticipated with mingled feelings of doubt and plain disbelief. Long a big singer in England, but virtually unknown here except through her London records, few expected her to live up to advance notices. But Miss Shelton wasn't halfway through her opening number when she proved she could sing. She also proved that she has one of the best voices around today, equally skilful with ballad or rhythm tune.

Gal opened fast with rhythmic *Shanghai* and hadn't gone beyond the first eight bars when she was in. Then a change of pace *Too Young* showing she knew what to do with a ballad, and the crowd was hers............Miss Shelton is a big blonde with a baby face. Her *Yiddishe Momma* may have been advised by somebody who told her the Copa crowd goes for it. Maybe it does, but Miss Shelton is too good a singer to do something maudlin to get to them, even though it was a big record in England. Incidentally, a few Dixieland arrangements for the band on *Some Of These Days* and *Mississippi* might add still more zest to an already outstanding singing performance.

Miss Shelton should go places in this country on voice alone. There's hardly a female singer in the pop field that can touch her.'

~*~

During Anne's visit to the States she had two hit records in the American Top Thirty. These were *Be Mine* and *Galway Bay* both these songs were also hits over here in the United Kingdom. Although Anne was travelling with her mother and fiancé, she was very home sick and missed her sisters, especially Josie, very much.

Whilst touring the States, Anne cut several discs that were released on the London Label; this was the American branch of

Decca Records. Sadly some of these recordings stayed on American shores and were never released over here, but they were very successful in the States for Anne. The arrangements for most of these songs were written by an extremely talented musician called Tutti Camarata, who had worked with many American stars including Bing Crosby, Frankie Lane, Bob Eberly, Helen Connor, and Louis Armstrong. He also worked with the orchestras of Tommy and Jimmy Dorsey. Tutti (or Toots as he was known by his friends) went on to play a big part in the lives of Anne and Jo that will be elaborated on later in the book.

So in December 1951, just before Christmas in fact 23rd December, Anne arrived home to the warmest welcome imaginable from her Dad, Jo and a five-month pregnant elder sister Eileen. Here follows an article from one of the daily papers that covered Anne's arrival home from the States. The picture mentioned with 'Christmas' the toy monkey is featured in the picture section of this book. (*Anne kept Christmas the monkey for forty years, but sadly he got lost when she moved to Sussex in 1994)

Singing Star is Home for Christmas dated 23rd December 1951.

"British singing star Anne Shelton displays her toy monkey named 'Christmas' which was a present from an oil millionaire that she has carried on 15,000 miles of tour. She is pictured in Southampton following her arrival from New York aboard the Canard *Queen Mary* today. Miss Shelton has become known as 'the star Americans want to keep'. She went to New York originally for a few months but she was overwhelmed with radio and television contracts and stayed for nearly a year. She cut her engagements short in order to be home for Christmas. In the New Year she will tour Britain with her own show"

Anne (this is where I want to say Patty) was so excited at the prospect of having another niece or nephew. The family were so pleased to be re-united, and I can imagine the stories there were to tell; what a wonderful Christmas that must have been, as I am sure once Anne Shelton crossed the threshold of her home, she became Patty, and would have been so happy to hang up 'Anne Shelton' in the wardrobe for a week or two!

After a welcomed rest at home, the New Year arrived, Anne was ready to start her mammoth schedule again and out came 'Anne Shelton' from the wardrobe.

The New Year was to be another fulfilling time for Anne, and also Eileen, who was due to give birth to her second child - me. Before I was born my name was decided upon, it was to be Kelly. This was not dependant on my being a girl, as it would have been the same name had I been a boy. The name was chosen by my Aunty Patty and my Nan when they were in the States the previous year. It was the name of one of Tutti Camarata's male relatives. His name, Kelly, was short for Carlton, and both Patty and Nan fell in love with the name, and persuaded mum that the new baby should be a Kelly! As it happened I was christened Althea Anne Kelly, as my parents thought Kelly was a bit too modern for a little girl in the 1950s. My dad did not have his way with choosing a name for me, as, due to the fact I was born on St George's Day (23rd April) and his name being George, he was rooting for Georgina, 'no way', thankfully, was that going to be allowed by the females in the family, (apologies to any Georgina's reading this biography, but Georgina is not a name I would have chosen for myself).

The day I was born, Patty was appearing in a show at Portsmouth, she insisted on being driven home after the show as she wanted to see Eileen and meet me! After our first meeting, we were as close as could be. My mum gave birth at home in my grandparents bedroom at 142 Court Lane, at 6.40am. I am still an early riser!

During 1952 Anne was very much in demand. She started the first of three series of a radio show called *Double Top* with Alfred Marks. It was a weekly show that began and ended with the song *I Have a Song*. Anne sang five or six songs during the show. The same year Anne also was featured in shows such as *Desert Island Discs*, *Henry Hall's Guest Night*, *Home at 8* and *Music Hall*. She also starred at the London Palladium on the 3rd, 10th and 17th October in the same year.

At this time, Anne's agent was Charles Tucker, of Charles Tucker Enterprises. Their offices were in Shaftsbury Avenue, London. Documentation that I recently found from the BBC shows that back in March 1953 Anne was paid a fee of £52.10 shillings for allowing the BBC 'to distribute records that she performed on *Variety Fanfare* (9th January 1953) to broadcasting stations situated overseas for reproduction by them' Anne had to agree to the following conditions-:

1. The Corporation and its assigns shall be entitled to all rights in the records of the programme, but it is understood that-:

a) The records will only be used for broadcasting purposes overseas;

b) The records will not be broadcast more than five times from any one transmitting aerial;

c) The records will not be sold to the public.

d) You undertake not to broadcast or to record for any other party any material provided by the Corporation and used by you in the programme.

We would like to make it clear that this use of the records is distinct from mechanical reproduction under your contract for the programme and in no way affects payment of any fees to which you are entitled under that contract for broadcasts of the records by the Corporation in its Home and Overseas Services'

Nice to see legally binding documents were just as hard to understand in those days as they are today.

Anne made so many records and broadcasts during the fifties that I would need to produce another book to cover them all. Anne could do no wrong, and the powers that be did everything they could to please her, everyone wanted her on their show, she was 'one hot potato' as our friends across the pond would say.

We now move onto 1956, a year that saw yet another change of recording label for Anne. She was now signed to Philips. I remember so well the Philips label, navy blue with two little stars in both the corners, funny the things that stay in your memory from childhood. This is the year where the very talented Johnnie Franz comes into Anne's life. He replaced Johnnie Spence as Anne's pianist, but also took on the role of her A&R (Artistes and Recording) manager. This was a relationship made in heaven. Johnnie was a genius. His arrangements of her songs complimented Anne's sound so well, they really were very fond of each other and had an excellent working relationship.

Johnnie was a frequent visitor to the family home in Dulwich; I remember his visits well, especially as I became a little older. One thing I do remember was that he always ate fresh prawns unshelled, heads and all. All he took off before he ate the prawn was the long whiskery bit by its eyes….amazing.

Anne had many hits with Decca, Rex and HMV including *I Remember The Cornfields*, *Galway Bay, Put Your Shoes On Lucy* (which by the way was the song she often sang me to sleep with when I was a baby) *Be Mine*, *Arrivederci Darling* and many more.

Soon Anne's career was to hit an all time high, as under the musical direction of Johnnie Franz, on the Philips label a song was released that would change her life forever, this was of course *Lay Down Your Arms*. This was Anne's one and only song to reach the number one slot in the hit parade. It stayed number one in the charts from September 21st 1956, until October 19th.

In the lead up to *Lay Down Your Arms* reaching the number one spot, Anne was really praying that it would get there. Here is a letter that she wrote to one of her fans, who went on to become a friend, Phyllis Kitchen. The lettercard was posted from East Dulwich, postmarked 4th September 1956.

"Dear Phil,

Here I am again, it is late and I am in bed so I thought I would write a few lines to you. We have been at the TV studios all day, not BBC but ATV. We are recording a show for the North only. It is called *The ATV Music Shop* and I'll be singing *Lay Down Your Arms*. It is going so well Phil, keep on praying it will get to the top please God. You know Phil, my dad always wanted me to get a number one disc.

Well dear, kiss your mum from me, my mummy is getting on so well thank God. I will write to you again soon, God Bless you and please excuse the scribble.

Love Anne'

(I would like to thank Phyllis for sending me this letter to copy, and for trusting me with it, as she has kept it safe for fifty years.....I have returned it undamaged!)

Anne did reach number one, and was so excited. She deserved to have this place as she had worked so hard. Here follows a short note that Anne received from Cecil Madden who was the head of the BBC (light programmes). It was dated 8th October 1956.

'Dear Anne.

Congratulations on being the top of the Hit Parade, no one deserves it more than you.

All wishes from your old boss........Cecil.

Her popularity was reflected by her four week stay at number one, and several weeks following in the charts. But there was a problem with the War Office; they were not in as much admiration of the song as were the rest of the country. When the song was released our country was in conflict once again by way of the Suez Crisis. The recording was thought to be inappropriate by some. Here follows an extract from *"Variety"* - New York, Sept 5th 1956.

"Arms' Subversive (London September 4th)

'Anne Shelton wanted to sing *Lay Down Your Arms* to troops at the National Radio Show on Tuesday (28th August) to plug her disking of the song. But the War Office turned down the idea because they thought the title and lyrics were 'too undignified' and subversive.

Full first line of the song, published by Francis, Day & Hunter is *Lay Down Your Arms and Surrender to Mine*. That sentiment apparently didn't appeal to the British Army.'

Despite the Home Office having concerns for the interpretation of the song, it did not stop the public from buying the record.

I would like to come out of the 1950s for a while to relate to you a correspondence that I received recently relating to *Lay Down Your Arms*. The following is an e-mail from a gentleman by the name of Chris Knight. I found its content most informative and interesting and I would like to share it with you.

'One of the best records I ever heard (and I still maintain to the present day) was *Lay Down Your Arms*. It just caught my imagination. I was eight or so when it came out and the production values, arrangement, lyrics and Anne's voice belting out that tune are brilliant. It was not for some years that I found out one of the reasons why I love that song. I am not sure if you have heard of the late British record producer Joe Meek who tragically died in 1967? He is best remembered for his recordings of *Telstar*, *Johnny Remember Me*, *Just Like Eddie* and *Have I the Right,* which were hits during the 60s. Before this in the 50s he was one of the most talented recording engineers and he was the engineer on *Lay Down Your Arms*. This song was memorable for its stomping military beat, an ingredient that helped to make it one of Miss Shelton's favourite recording sessions. Here follows Anne's own account of the making of *Lay Down Your Arms*.

"We had lots of laughs. We did a couple of rehearsals for balance then the producer Johnnie Franz, decided that we needed marching feet. My husband David suggested that we went down to the Wellington Barracks to bring some soldiers back and have them marching up and down in the studio. Joe said, "and I'll make the tea." Of course we all started laughing, then Joe went on to say, "I can give you the effect of marching feet." To which Johnnie

Franz replied, "Yes, we can get a record or tape." Joe said, "No, no I can get you the same effect that you would get on the radio of real marching men". Shortly afterwards he came back in with a box of gravel then someone (Adrian Kerridge) stood between me shaking this box backwards and forwards. We did two takes and when the session was finished I remember that the new black suit I was wearing was covered in white dust which had come out of the box."

The above quote came from the book *The Legendary Joe Meek-The Telstar Man* written by John Repsch.

Amazingly Joe Meek was tone deaf. He was a colourful, if not troubled young man. He once claimed to have made contact with Buddy Holly during a séance. He was also the first producer to record Tom Jones and Screaming Lord Sutch. A true original, he was Britain's first independent record producer. He made futuristic tunes that caught the imagination of the swinging 60s. This young man sadly met a very tragic end on 3rd February 1967, at the age of 37, Joe shot his landlady dead then killed himself.

~*~

1956 held two big happenings for Anne, one was her success in the charts and the other was sadly the death of her father. His death was not expected and came as a great shock to the family. He had not been ill, nor had he shown any signs of any ailments, in fact he was a very active man. The day that he died Anne, David and her mother, were away in Ipswich where Anne was appearing in a theatre in the city centre. Josie was at home with her dad, who was left to care for her as she was recovering from whooping cough. The month was June, it was very warm, Josie's dad told her that he wanted to take a stroll in the garden as it was such a beautiful evening, but she best stay inside as she had not been well and he did not want her to catch a cold.

He kissed her on the forehead and went for his stroll. After about an hour, Josie became anxious as he had not returned. She got out of bed and took off into the garden to look for him. The garden was huge, over an acre. She took the path to the side of a very large privet hedge that lead to the vegetable patch. There she saw her dad lying on the ground, face down. My granddad was a big man, but Josie, who was slight, managed to roll him over onto his back. She could not wake him and was about to try and blow air into his mouth, but stopped as she was frightened she might infect him with her whooping cough.

She ran back to the house and phoned my mum and dad who lived just across the lane. Josie and my mum Eileen went to their dad but he was dead. Both now so upset, traumatised and in a state of shock, had to prepare themselves to pass this devastating news to their mum and Anne. On receiving the news Anne and her mother returned from Ipswich that night. Anne went back the next day to perform, but drove back every night for the rest of the week after each show. The family were devastated. The reason why Anne carried on performing in Ipswich was because, she said, that "her dad would have wanted her to fulfil her contract and not to let her fans down who had paid to see her". She was playing to a full house every night. Knowing what a family orientated woman she was, I know how hard it would have been for her to have left her mum and sisters alone at home at such a time. One cannot imagine what professionalism it would have taken for her to go and perform under such circumstances.

Granddad was buried at Brenchley Gardens, Forest Hill in London. He was only 67 when he died of a massive heart attack.

My Granddad had a colourful collection of neckties and, as a little girl, I loved ties. I remember crying as all the family were going to 'Grangrags' (as I called him) funeral and I had to stay at home with a child minder. To placate me, my mum and aunts said I could have all Granddad's ties to play with; problem solved. The innocence of youth! I did not know what a funeral was, all I knew was that Grangrag had gone to see Jesus and it was making everyone cry a lot.

Six weeks later Anne had another traumatic episode. Her mother was rushed to hospital having collapsed. Again, Anne was away appearing in a variety show in St Leonards, East Sussex. She travelled every day to visit her mum who was in a London nursing home. The newspaper headlines read *Anne sings through double tragedy, but the show must go on.*

Anne was now the only breadwinner in the family, but thankfully she was in a position to be able to support them all.

It is sad to think that Anne's father who had been so instrumental in pushing Anne forward and supporting her all through her career, did not live to see her reach the number one spot in the hit parade with *Lay Down Your Arms.*

At this time probably due to a combination of influences Anne lost a tremendous amount of weight and became quite streamline. There was an article featured in *The People's Journal* dated 4th August 1956, that states that Anne had lost five stone, dropping to eleven stone from sixteen. She put it down to willpower and a controlled diet, cutting out fats and sweets. It mentions how the diet was monitored by a doctor in Harley Street. This would imply that she may well have decided to take some dieting pill to help her, even if this was the case, she did very well to keep the weight off for many years. The stress of losing her father might have also been a contributing factor to the weight loss.

The next event that I would like to tell you about, might seem somewhat out of character for Anne and I must say that I believe, in this particular incident, that she was somewhat influenced by her fiancé David, who had established himself as her manager.

Perhaps this would be a good time to give you an update on family life in Dulwich. Anne's father was dead and her mother was even more in control of the family. She suffered very noticeable mood swings, as a little girl she frightened me. She was always shouting and often upset her three daughters. My mum was not living at home any longer as my parents had their own home, albeit across the road from Glendower no more than a hundred yards away, but mum still visited her sisters daily, much to the annoyance of my dad. I would often be at Glendower and hear my Nan shouting and becoming very angry with everyone, more often than not it was David, Anne's fiancé that took the brunt.

She believed that he should not be earning his living from Anne as her manager, but should be out in the world earning an independent wage. I think she was jealous of the fact that she did not have complete control of Anne as she once had. This might make my aunt sound weak and bullied, but this was not the case, she never retaliated or argued, as she was always the peacemaker, she always wanted everything to be all right and for there to be no quarrelling. Sometimes when there was a barney going on, nearly always instigated by Nan, she would take me away upstairs to the third floor and read me a story. We went to the top of the house, as that was far enough away from the 'war zone' that you could not hear the shouting. She was always there to protect me and I always felt so safe with her. When I was sad she used to talk to me sounding like Donald Duck, she had the ability to mimic that duck! It always made me laugh and she could carry on talking like it for so long.

So now that I have explained to you the family situation at this time, I will go on to tell you the happening that caused Anne to take such indignation at the proposal offered by the BBC.

In May 1958 Bryan Sears, a BBC producer suggested a proposal to the powers that be that a programme co-starring Anne Shelton and Alma Cogan, should be considered. He went on to say in his letter to the Light Entertainments Office:

"I saw these two artists in a commercial production a little while ago in which they both worked together in an ad-lib manner extremely well. As neither of these charming performers is given to an excess of strong drink it was obviously a natural joie de vivre.

In this show they made fun of each other very charmingly and I feel that singing both separately and together and introducing guests, we could have a lot of very uninhibited good clean humour."

This show with Anne and Alma co-starring together was given the thumbs up and all seemed to be going well, with the potential for a very successful series. Sadly all did not go well. The reason - Anne was billed lower down than Alma. David, Anne's manager/fiancé, was furious and insisted Anne bow out of the programme. His rationale was that Anne was a big star and Alma hadn't been on the scene all that long and was not exactly a polished singer and did not warrant top billing. At this time Anne had changed agents from Charles Tucker to Billy Marsh, a part of the Delfont Agency. He also felt that the intended billing was an insult to Anne and backed her (or David's) decision. So, Anne again not wanting to cause an upset and probably feeling a little put out herself wrote the following letter to Francis Essex, at the BBC, on the 16th June 1958.

"My dear Francis,

You will by now have heard from Billy Marsh that I have decided not to appear in the show with Alma Cogan. I do hope that this decision has not inconvenienced you greatly. But for me to appear under such circumstances would only cause me unhappiness. This I know you would not want.

I must confess however, that I am not amused at the Publicity Department regarding my billing.

I am sure that such a large Corporation as the BBC realise the importance of same to an artiste, and it appears extraordinary to me that such an important decision as this could be decided by 'the toss of a coin'. Enough of my worries Francis, I would like to thank you again for inviting me to appear on your show and hope that I may have the pleasure of working with you in the near future without such disturbances to worry us.

                              Yours sincerely
                              Anne."

The response from Anne's (or maybe David's) letter to Francis follows…..

"My dear Anne,

Thank you very much for you letter dated 16th June, and do forgive me for not replying earlier, a number of crisis (this being one of them) have kept me rather busy.

I need hardly say how upset I am at your decision to withdraw from my show this coming Saturday and even more upset perhaps that you took this course without the telephone call that you promised when I rang you on Friday 13th June.

I must express great surprise that you have adopted this attitude that we decided billing at a 'toss of a coin'. This of course is not only inaccurate but quite absurd. I find the suggestion that we should treat our star artists in this way quite un-called for. I spent a considerable time explaining to you my reasons for billing you second to Alma Cogan, and you assured me that you understood and even explained away your agent's threats to me in the afternoon.

However, I do not think much will be gained by continuing a useless argument. I can only say once again how disappointed I am at your decision.

My best wishes.
Francis Essex"

Well I must say you can read into that what you like, but it does sound that the letter from Anne was not written without influence from another, as it was out of character for her. The strange thing is that Anne and Alma went on to be good friends, and they appeared together a year or so later when nearly all the top British female singers were chosen for a Royal Variety Show. These lady artists included Anne, Eve Boswell, Ruby Murray, Joan Regan and Alma Cogan. They did a couple of sketches together and it so happened that Anne and Alma were next to each other and were both wearing crinoline type dresses (as were the others) and were carrying parasols. In the routine the ladies had to split in the middle of the formation, with one group going off to the left, the other to the right. Anne was to turn right and was paired with Alma who was to turn left, unfortunately, Anne's parasol was caught up inside Alma's crinoline and neither could move freely. This caused a huge laugh with great applause from the audience. Whether it was rehearsed or not, we will never know.

I would like to just take some time to mention Alma Cogan and her all too short life. She was born Alma Angela Cohen on the 19th May 1932 in Stepney, London. She was the sister to the actress Sandra Caron. As mentioned, despite their somewhat turbulent early encounter, Anne and Alma became good friends and Anne respected Alma as a performer. It must have been hard for my aunt as she was famed for previous decades in show business and Alma it must be said, was somewhat taking over Anne's position, and becoming the future star. In the 60s, Alma had a close relationship with the Beatles manager Brian Epstein, both coming from a strong Jewish background. Brian was a homosexual, so there were no romantic ties. Alma went on to be a big star and was noted to often change her dresses up to eleven times in a show. Her star status was not to last for long, as she sadly lost her life to cancer and died on the 26th October 1966 at the age of 34. My aunt Anne was very saddened by her death.

Anne had other chart entries whilst recording with Philips. These were *The Village of St Bernadette, Seven Days* and *Sailor.* There was another single around at the same time originating from Italy, *Volare.* This song was recorded by many artists both in this country and America. Anne's rendition did not reach the number one spot, although she did enjoy good sales from the record. The most popular recording of *Volare* was that of Dean Martin (must have been his Italian connection) another great singer.

After a while LPs (Long Playing Records) were introduced attracting many sales. These records soon became more popular than the single, as they were better value for money. Anne's first LP was released in 1958 and was entitled *The Shelton Sound;* Anne was accompanied by the Wally Stott Orchestra. There were some wonderful tracks on the album such as, *Happiness Is A Thing Called Joe, All Of A Sudden My Heart Sings, Smoke Gets In Your Eyes* and many more, twelve in total. I must say that with Wally Stott's arrangements and Anne's interpretation of those songs this album is still one of my favourites, such artistry from both of them.

Anne's second LP was entitled *Songs From the Heart* which is just what they were, a very popular collection of songs, including *As Time Goes By, Sand In My Shoes* and '*But Not For Me*. She was yet again accompanied by Wally Stott and her own pianist Johnny Franz.

There is an interesting and true story about how Johnny Franz introduced Anne to the idea of her second LP. He invited her into the studio to talk over some new arrangements that he had done for her. Later, they strolled across the road to a café where Anne ordered one of her favourite tipples, a glass of milk. Johnny intervened saying 'Oh no Anne, don't have milk, have a cup of coffee'. He did this knowing that she never drank milk before a recording session and Johnny had a trick up his sleeve! He told her that the reason he suggested she did not have the milk was that he may want her to go over a few numbers later. When back at the studio, Johnny asked Anne if she would have a word with the conductor Wally Stott when he arrived. As soon as Wally appeared he handed Anne a bundle of arrangements and said 'Anne Shelton, This is your Life' The studio were all set to record her second LP, all except Anne who knew nothing about it, but as always she took it all in her stride and amazingly the recording went through without a hitch. She did have other LPs released through the years, but these mostly were a compilation of previously recorded singles.

Wally Stott was born in Leeds in 1924. He was a transsexual and underwent sex reassignment surgery in the 1970s. She is now known as Angela Morley and lives in Arizona. Angela is still a great composer and is well known for writing the theme tune and incidental music for *Hancock's Half Hour* and also wrote and conducted music for *The Goon Show*, and most of the score for *Watership Down*. Angela was awarded three Emmys for her work in television musical scoring.

Before we leave the 50s I would like to share a few more stories with you. The first I think you will find amusing. Let me take you back to the Finsbury Park Theatre in London, to a rehearsal, or band call as it was often called. On the bill with

Anne were Mike and Bernie Winters, who as you may well remember were an English double act who were very popular from the mid 50s to the early 70s. Bernie Winters (the more amusing of the two) always had his St Bernard dog with him called Schnorbitz, (I do believe there must have been several Schnorbitzs during the years, as Bernie still featured the dog twenty years down the line) At this particular rehearsal all the music to be used for the various artists acts was laid out on the floor of the stage, in order of their appearance. The time came to break for lunch and everyone went their separate ways. Somehow Schnorbitz wandered out of Bernie's dressing room onto the stage. After having a good old sniff around, he decided that he would take a pee over Anne's music. I am sure my aunt would have understood, as she was a great animal lover and when you have to go, you have to go! It caused screams of laughter from one and all who were present; mostly I am sure from Anne. The brothers split in the 70s over a disagreement and never worked together again. Bernie died in 1991 aged just 58 of stomach cancer. His brother Mike (or 'choochie face' as Bernie often called him) is still alive living in the States.

In May 1957 the great Sophie Tucker made one of her rare visits to this country. On the 9th of May that year, Jack Hylton presented a show called *Lady Ratlings on Parade*. The Lady Ratlings were the female equivalent of the *Grand Order of Water Rats,* which is still an organisation supported by many show business stars who work tirelessly for different charities. Anne shared top billing with Sophie, who insisted that Anne join her in singing *One Of These Days* (this was one of Miss Tuckers greatest hits, which she first performed in America back in the 20s) the show was televised on AR-TV and was a great success. It has been recorded that after the show Sophie Tucker said 'I will never be dead whilst Anne Shelton is around' their style and deliverance of a song was most compatable.

Again in the late 50s Anne was appearing at the Prince of Wales Theatre in the West End of London with the legendry Lonnie Donegan, well known for his rather loud rendition of music known as skiffle, which was Lonnie's version of American Folk Music. At this particular show my mum and dad were in the audience. My dad, who owned a chain of butcher shops, was up most mornings by 3am to enable him to be at Smithfield meat market by 4am. As you can imagine by the evening he was very tired, so this evening was no exception.

After Lonnie had finished his performance he went back to Anne's dressing room, as he would often do, and said to her, "You will never believe it Annie, there's this bald headed bloke in the front row, who slept all through my act." Anne just knew there and then it was her brother-in-law George. She never ever admitted that to Lonnie!

In 1957 The Anne Shelton Fan Club was formed and was run with the assistance of three very able ladies, May Smethurst, for the fans in the north of England, Kathleen Judkins, for those in southern counties, and last but by no means least, Phyllis Kitchen for those fans in the Midlands. It was very successful and had many members across the country. It also was very useful for fans wanting information about recordings, dates for future shows and anything else that Anne was taking part in. Solving a problem for Anne as far as correspondence was concerned, as she made a point of not answering fan letters personally, because of the time factor involved, but she made sure that the regular newsletters were published and distributed by the club secretaries. The three ladies, May, Kathleen and Phyllis were dedicated to their job as Anne's representatives and did admirable work. I am still in contact with May and Phyllis but sadly do not know the whereabouts of Kathleen. Anne was also in contact with the three until her death.

During the 50s Anne not only toured America and Europe but also visited South Africa, Canada and Hong Kong. She also topped the bill in every leading variety theatre in the UK. In 1959 and 1960 she was honoured to be chosen to appear in the Royal Variety Show, and went on to do a great number of charity shows with the Royal family present.

We are now moving into the swinging 60s. In my opinion this is when Anne was at her professional best.

Chapter Five

The Swinging Sixties…..and Anne was still swinging.

I really do not know where to start with this chapter. I guess at the start of the decade might be a good idea, it is just that so much happened to Anne at this time both professionally and personally that I want to make sure I don't miss anything.

It was in the 60s that I started to spend most of my time with Patty (Anne, in case you have forgotten). Anne had changed from the young inexperienced schoolgirl who started in the 40s to become a mature, attractive woman. I have so many personal memories and stories to tell that I could go on forever, but I will try and keep my accounts interesting, factual and hopefully amusing.

The 60s was a time of change, a time long past, but not forgotten. It was the era of James Bond, Elvis Presley, The Beatles, The Cold War, Hippies and many things too numerous to mention, but Anne Shelton was still holding on in there.

At the start of the 60s the biggest change to television was the introduction of Commercial TV as an alternative to the BBC, which had held the monopoly for many years.

Anne was invited to take part in numerous shows on the 'new' channel, some of which were her own and others where she was a guest artist.

I found a memo from the BBC dated 20th July 1960, suggesting Anne as a replacement for Vera Lynn. It is interesting to see how much money she was paid in those days, probably not as much in comparison to the 'talented' artists of today.

"From: Assistant Television Booking Manager, 2139 T.C.
Subject: ANNE SHELTON
To: C.T.   Copies to: C.P.Tel: H.P.P.

As a replacement for the Vera Lynn series we are hoping to engage Anne Shelton for thirteen weekly programmes between October 3rd and December 26th, and an option for a further thirteen weeks to be completed before the end of June 1961. We intend to offer her 250 guineas per show with a rise to 300 guineas per show if the option is taken up for the last thirteen programmes, but we may be forced to pay her 300 guineas for the first thirteen shows and 350 for the other thirteen. This we do not consider exorbitant but should be our top figure.

May I have your authority to negotiate along these lines please?

Signed: Bush Bailey

Noted across this memo was an agreement from....? Sadly I cannot read the signature but his comment was 'Yes, Miss Lynn is experiencing difficulties; I think this is a good replacement.'

In February 1960 Anne undertook another tour to South Africa, appearing at Ciros Johannesburg for two weeks, then she went on to appear for a week in Durban and a further week in Southern Rhodesia. She also found time to appear in two concerts on behalf of the Israeli-Jewish League. The tour was very exhausting and lasted about six weeks.

Not only were there more shows appearing due to the new television channel, but also additional radio programmes becoming available with new stations like Radio Luxemburg and Radio Caroline (which by the way were 'pirate' stations and operated off shore, which was strictly speaking illegal). One of Anne's first Radio Luxemburg programmes began in October 1958 and was called *The Anne Shelton Song Parade* with the Geoff Love Orchestra accompanying her. It was scheduled to run for more than six months. There was a further series in 1961 when thirteen half hour programmes were recorded from various towns and cities. These shows had an invited audience.

Geoff Love was another talented composer, musical director. He was born in Yorkshire in 1917. He worked with Anne and many artists including Connie Francis, Russ Conway, Judy Garland, Frankie Vaughan and Marlene Dietrich. With his orchestra he also became very popular for his easy listening sound of music.

Another show that Anne was invited onto was called *Laughline*. It sounded really good. Here follows yet another letter from the BBC, dated 6th January 1961.

"Dear Miss Shelton,

I am enclosing the six cartoons to be included in *Laughline* on Tuesday 17th January. This programme is to be tele-recorded on Sunday 15th January at the Television Theatre, Shepherds Bush, and we would be very glad to see you about 3.30pm.

We should like you to contribute a laughline to each of the cartoons. The rules are quite simple: the characters in the cartoon can be moved into any position that you wish, and all properties seen in the drawing can be utilised in any manner you require. The only limitations are that the characters must not be sent off the stage, nor may their wardrobe be altered, as this would be departing from the original drawing. If you feel you would like to add a few personal props not already in these drawings, please let us know what you have in mind so that we may order them in time. Also, should you have any difficulty regarding the laughline for any particular cartoon, please do not hesitate to tell us and we will do our best to help.

We should be extremely grateful to hear your ideas if possible a few days before the tele-recording, and we look forward to seeing you on Sunday 15th.

Yours sincerely: G.B. Lupino

Don't you think that sounds like a good show? I wonder if any of you reading this remember it.

1961 also saw Anne with her own series on the BBC. Anne was very focused on what she wanted in the show and had several meetings with the powers that be to discuss the layout and content. One of these meetings was with Duncan Wood who was the Chief Assistant, (Light Entertainment) and John Humphreys. Here are the points and concerns, that were raised at the meeting, and were sent to the head of Light Entertainment.

"Anne has been extremely worried about the prospect of doing forty-five minutes of pure requests, and I don't think it is feasible to expect her to carry the show on this selling point alone. Obviously requests will form the backbone of the series, but we must present a show first and foremost.

The number of requests in each programme should be about five or six. One of these, the final request, would involve Anne herself, either by film or live, meeting and talking to the person involved. The remainder will be film of one kind or another of the person making the request only.

Anne is very keen to work with Irving Davies. Ryan Sears endorses this thought. It is proposed therefore that Irving should be resident choreographer on the show, and he would be responsible for the production numbers and for choreographic interpretation of some requests.

She felt that her working with the small rhythm group on the last *Friday Show* was a successful idea, and she would like to continue this as a regular spot in the series. Since this is reasonably inexpensive and makes a change musically, I think this would be a good idea.

It was agreed that Harry Rabinowitz should be the Musical Director. This is possible from our schedules and, I would think, desirable from our point of view.

There would be a small resident group of dancers, about six. There would also be a small resident vocal group and we all felt that it would be a good thing to use some new faces in this.

The budget for this show is £2000. Employing the above points in the programme format and assuming one or two guests per show, plus a film effort costing £250 -£300 per show, the budgeting is likely to be tight. However Bryan Sears realises that the programme must be achieved within this figure and when both he and Anne Shelton have had further thoughts, he will submit a more detailed format".

The series went ahead in July 1961 and was called *Ask Anne*. As planned Anne talked to members of the public who had made requests. In one show she interviewed a woman in the audience whose name was Anne Shelton, I bet that was interesting.

One of Anne's guests was her sister Jo, who had recently started in show business as a singer. She was also a very talented dancer and performed a song and dance routine on the show with Irving Davies.

Anne also had a show on Associated Redifussion (the other side) in which both Anne and Jo appeared together, this was *The Anne Shelton Show*.

Jo made her TV debut in November 1958 and was introduced by Anne. Jo later admitted that she was sick with nerves, but as always Anne was by her side to see her through. Jo was very talented; she had such a similar voice to Anne, both contraltos. They also had similar speaking voices and on the phone one was often mistaken for the other. Anne was always Jo's greatest fan, and gave her so much support. Jo once said in interview; "Anne is my favourite singer, she is so versatile. Her voice has a bigger range than mine, a much richer quality and such fantastic control". Anne promptly replied with; "My voice may have more power that's all. Jo is so reliable. We always seek each other's opinion on songs and we encourage each other." This was very true; they were so close in all things.

This seems like a good time to talk about Jo's career, which sadly did not last long, albeit from her own choosing. For years Jo's family had been encouraging her to follow in Anne's footsteps but she chose not to. It was not until she was twenty-three when fate persuaded her to use her voice professionally. One evening, Anne's agent Billy Marsh was invited to attend a family evening to celebrate their mother's birthday. Whilst he was there he heard

Jo's voice on a family tape, he was so impressed that he insisted on booking her to appear with Anne on her variety tour. In the show they sang a duet, significantly called *Friendship*.

Jo went on to appear in a summer season with Anne in 1958. She was then invited by Dicky Leeman to perform in *A Music Shop*. Jo was reluctant to do this as it was her first solo performance, before she had always performed with Anne. Jo's other TV performances were in *The Benny Hill Show, Sunday Night at The Prince of Wales* and a Cyril Stapleton series.

It was thought by many that Jo made a mistake in using the same surname as Anne. Some said she had done it to try and further her career, and others thought the name Shelton was too much for her to live up too. Anne disagreed with both of these statements and said, "The important thing is to live up to the name and this Jo is doing."

Jo carried on performing into the mid sixties, but retired from show business to take care of their mother who was not in good health. It was such a shame. I have always felt that it was a waste of a great talent. Jo always put every member of her family's needs before her own, right up to her death in 1991.

People were beginning to holiday once again in good old England, mainly choosing seaside resorts that during the war had been out of bounds, due to the threat of enemy invasion. One of the most popular resorts was Blackpool with its mile of golden sand and an abundance of theatres, many of which were at the end of the pier. They were all offering great entertainment in seasonal variety shows.

Anne did many summer seasons in these resorts, including Blackpool, and always had top billing. These *Summer Seasons* as they were called usually ran for three months. This meant that Anne and her entourage needed to rent a property for the duration of the season. I remember these times so well. As a child I spent my school summer holidays with her which usually meant going to some seaside town. I remember Blackpool well. She rented a big house by the sea and we had such fun there. I was often with her, as my mum and dad were in business in London and could not leave, so my aunts became my second mums, or "mothers on holiday" as I used to call them.

Life was great in those days. Looking back my aunt must have been so tired, as she always got up reasonably early to spend the day with me and then I would go with her to the theatre in the evening. My Nan, Jo and David were always with Anne on these tours and often the need arose for her to drive back to London for a show or broadcast, then dash back up north the same day.

Staying with those happy days for a while, as mentioned Anne did many summer seasons, often it would just be Anne, David and me. We always stayed in five star hotels. My aunt was always recognised, which I loved, and was always being asked for her autograph. We used to return to the hotel late in the evening after the show. The three of us would make our way to the hotel restaurant where there was always a cold buffet left for us. It seemed really funny to me then, to be the only people in the dimly lit dining area, it was all so very exciting. The meal usually consisted of cold meat, salads and bread rolls, Patty and I always had Cola, David had a whiskey. It always smelled so posh, Patty's perfume was very strong and I loved it, in fact I wear it today Jean Pateau's *Joy,* it reminds me still of the smell of back stage and the excitement of being there. Patty and I shared a suite and poor old Uncle David had a separate room.

Featured in one of these summer shows at Blackpool was a fairly new star named Terry Hall, a ventriloquist who had acquired a new dummy. Terry paid a fortune to have it made. We are of course talking about *Lenny the Lion.* His first performance with Lenny turned out to be a complete flop and he barely received any applause. Terry, understandably felt most dejected. Anne was standing in the wings, having watched his performance. She consoled him and told him that he must not give up. She then suggested to Terry that maybe he should change Lenny's voice to something coyer, not so gruff and serious. She then went on to demonstrate what she meant. Anne was wonderful with changing her voice and could also speak in any accent. She really had a great talent to mimic.

Terry took Anne's advice and worked on a new voice for the lion. His next appearance was a great success and he came off to rapturous applause. He could not thank Anne enough and she as always was just happy to be able to help.

On the 9th December 1961, Anne gave a party, which was held at the Napoleon Suite at the fashionable Café Royal, Regent Street, London to celebrate her 21st year in show business. Anne invited all her fans to dine with her and then went on to perform a cabaret for them. She was accompanied on the piano by Johnny Franz, and not only did she sing songs that she had recently recorded, but also many others by request from the fans present. Anne stood on one of the very plush upholstered chairs so that she could see everybody, and everyone could see her. I was at the celebration, as was another Anne, the daughter of a dear friend Jim Woolley. Both Anne and I were nine years old, and it was her birthday that day. My aunt made everyone stand up and sing happy birthday to her.

The 60s were really a very good time for Anne professionally, she was at the height of her career and there was no sign of her popularity decreasing. Despite the changing influences on the music scene, Anne and her very distinctive style was still very much in demand.

In 1963 she was invited by Yul Brynner, who was acting on behalf of the United Nations to perform a song on a unique record that was to be produced in aid of the World's refugees. Anne felt honoured to be asked and she agreed to take part along with Edith Piaf, Nat King Cole, and many other artists of different nationalities. Anne was representing England, and sang *Greensleeves*. The record was issued by United Nations high commissioner for refuges, it was very successful, and went on to sell over a million copies. For this Anne received a gold disc, which was presented to her by Yul Brynner. On the disc, which I am proud to say is now hanging in my study, is inscribed:

'All Star Festival'
Golden Record presented to Anne Shelton
On the occasion of the sale of the first million
June 1963

As I mentioned earlier Jo had given up her idea of any future in show business to become a carer to their mother whose health was failing. I never really knew what was wrong with my Nan, but looking back to that time now, she was obviously suffering from senile dementia. When I think what a strong willed, dominating woman she had been, to see her like a helpless little child was very sad. Anne was as always working and often away from home leaving Jo and Eileen to care for their mum. The task was very demanding and was beginning to take its toll on Jo. After many distressing months my Nan died on 4th June 1965. My mum and aunts were with her when she passed away. I was kept home from school that day, and I was so sad that she had died, and even more saddened to see how upset Mum, Patty and Josie were.

Nan's coffin was placed in the lounge and remained open until the day of her funeral. I was asked if I wanted to say goodbye to her. I must admit I was a little frightened, as being only thirteen I had never seen a dead person before. I thought that out of respect I should. Patty, Josie and mum came in with me. Patty was holding my hand as we went into the room. The first thing that struck me was the strong smell of cucumber; I have since found out that it must have been the embalming fluid. I approached the coffin that was surrounded by many burning candles. Nan looked very peaceful, as if she was asleep. I was not at all scared.

The funeral, with a full requiem mass took place in the chapel at my school, Virgo Fidelis Convent in Norwood, south east London. The service was very moving, as in those days the mass was in Latin and the nuns sang most of the responses. Nan was buried with her husband at Brenchley Gardens.

Anne Shelton's (and Patty Sibley's) life would never be the same again. It must have been a terrible wrench to loose her mother, Lamma, as she had been with her from the very start of her career. Jo now took on the role of constant companion to Anne, replacing her mum, so that the Anne Shelton entourage now consisted of Jo and David. It took them a long time to get over her death; in fact, I don't think they ever did.

I would like to tell you now about a very good friend of the family and his very sad end. I am talking about Freddie Mills the boxer. Freddie and his family were all close to us. Chrissie, his wife was best friends with my mum Eileen, Susan his eldest daughter was the same age as me, and we became childhood friends, spending a lot of time in each other's houses after school. He had another daughter Mandy who was about five years younger than us. Freddie himself was everyone's friend, especially close to Anne, Jo and David. Many a day and evening was spent together, always with so much laughter. I remember Freddie always wore some lovely jewellery. He was always so smart and often wore crocodile shoes. He was very much a showman. He used to pick up his girls from school in his large Citroen saloon car and often gave loads of kids a lift home. The Mills family lived in a large family house about three miles from Glendower, their address, was 186 Denmark Hill.

I am sure my aunt would be pleased that I am mentioning Freddie in her biography, as they were close and the whole family were saddened and shocked by his tragic death.

Freddie was born on 26th June 1919 in Poole. He was the World Light Heavyweight Champion from 1948 until 1950. It was his durability and determination, as well as his boxing skills that took him to the pinnacle of his career. He lost his heavyweight title on January 24th 1950 in London to a boxer called Joey Maxim.

His face was frequently on television, and he appeared in films from 1952 until 1965. Two of which were *Carry on Regardless* and *Carry on Constable*. As well as his career in show business, he also started a business venture, which turned out to be his downfall. Freddie joined up with a Chinese businessman and he became co-owner of a London Night Club/Chinese Restaurant in Soho. His partner was the business brain behind it and Freddie was the front man.

Freddie enjoyed a very expensive life style. He was a very generous man and spent a lot of money on gifts for his family and friends. As a child he once bought me a junior size punch ball and boxing gloves. A strange present for a little girl you might say, but

I was rather a tomboy. In fact my dad who was an amateur boxer taught me several moves when I was little, Freddie thought that was wonderful, hence the gift. I had a picture that was taken of Freddie and me with the punch ball, which appeared in a local paper, but sadly I no longer have it.

Things were not going well for Freddie financially. He had tax debts and had lost a lot of his fortune. On July 25th 1965, on a back street in Soho, Freddie was found dead in the back of his car with a shotgun wound to his head.

David, who was one of the first people to be alerted to his death said that the shotgun was by the side of Freddie's leg, and both his hands were on his lap. This implies he shot himself, and then put his hands back on his lap? The police said it was suicide, but this is something his family and my family never believed.

Freddie was afraid of dying and hated anything to do with death. I remember my aunt saying that when her mum died the month before, Freddie and Chrissie came over to the house, he was asked if he wanted to say farewell to mum, (as he always called my Nan) his response was quite dramatic. There was no way he wanted to see anyone in a coffin, as he was scared by it all, hardly the response from a man contemplating suicide. Another reason why we believe he did not kill himself was that he loved his wife and children so much. They were his life and he would not have hurt them like that and leave them in so much pain and financial trouble. Freddie had plenty of friends who would have helped him financially, Anne being one.

Freddie died under a cloud of mystery. There have been several explanations put forward, some of them so farfetched and spiteful that I choose not to give them mention. The views of many who knew Freddie well were that he was under pressure from gangsters to pay protection money to them for his club. This he refused to do and Freddie was found dead.

The song that will always remind me of that time is *Help* by The Beatles. Funny how there is always a musical link to such memories.

Freddie Mills was a gentle giant. His large, strong frame held a tender heart of gold. He was the original big softie.

Anne and Jo had suffered the loss of two people close to them within two months of each other, but life carried on as usual in the family home, albeit without the dominance of their mother.

There were many live shows, tours abroad, television appearances and recording contracts that kept coming in for Anne, it kept her near the top of the ladder, even though she may have dropped a few rungs.

We must remember here how much the music scene had change. America's influence and the changing modern era were upon us. Rock 'n' Roll was showing signs of collapse but still carrying over from the 50s were Elvis Presley, Roy Orbison, The Everly Brothers and others, but on both continents older 'pop' stars were fading away as they struggled to find material that would 'click' with this energetic new generation of kids.

Pop Music (as it was so delightfully referred to, must say I always thought pop was a fizzy drink) was becoming controlled by new young 'vocal' groups who were showing new and various talents including the writing of their own material. Eventually rock/pop artists came to be expected to write and even produce their own songs, and it would be considered a failure if they could not do so.

Just a few examples of the new entertainers were The Beatles, Rolling Stones, Beach Boys and so many more, in fact the list of those considered to have talent in those days was endless and there are not enough pages in this book for me to cover them all. Although I must say that most of the music recorded on the Motown label was something else. This was a sound that I was hooked on, as were surprisingly, Anne and Jo in later years.

It is interesting to note that Anne, despite the tremendous change in music taste, managed to pull a full attendance at her performances for many years to come.

During the 60s and indeed into the 70s there was a very popular programme called *Juke Box Jury*. Anne was often one of the panel members. For those of you who might not remember the show, I will enlighten you to the format. There was a panel of celebrities (usually three) that were invited to give their opinions on newly released songs. On this occasion it was one of Anne's records being reviewed and the panel which consisted of Arthur Askey, Ted Ray and the American newcomer Johnny Mathis, the song that was being reviewed was *The Carnival is Closed Today*. Sadly the American showed little, if no restraint at being rude and insulting about Anne. He mistakenly went on to say when asked his opinion that "Anne sounded like a tired Jo Stafford, and the song was rubbish." The response to his comments, must have been uplifting to Anne, as Arthur Askey (a friend of Anne's) pounced on him and said "You should be ashamed of yourself as a special guest on this programme insulting one of our best loved lady singers." Ted Ray went on to say, "You are perfectly entitled to say you don't like the record, but the rest of your unfounded comments were definitely out of order.

It would appear Mr Mathis was put well and truly in his place. I must say I think *The Carnival is Closed Today* was a great song, as good as any of his.

There was another song due to be released in November 1969 that Anne had recorded under the musical direction of the so talented Tutti Camarata. Here follows an Inter-Office Communication from Walt Disney Music Company (America)

To: Frank Weintrop

From: Jimmy Johnson   Date: October 23rd 1969

Dear Frank.

Since I understand you were touring the continent when Tutti made the recording of *It Won't be Long Till Christmas* with Anne Shelton, you have a thrill in store for you when you play the enclosed dub. The backing will be the *Christmas Star*, which is also a beautiful tune, but there is no question about which should be the A side of this single.

We plan on releasing the single in this country (America) in the first week in November and it will be enclosed in an attractive four color sleeve. Because this song is something more than just a Christmas tune and because of the title we feel we have a good chance to secure airplay in this country during November and won't have to wait for the limited period of time in December. We would like you to do the same thing in the UK.This is an unabashedly sentimental song and in today's market it is not going to be easy to break through with this record. However, with plenty of hard work I think we can do it and if we do succeed we will have a standard that will go on for years.

Billy Marsh, who is Anne's close associate and who is mixed up with ATV is tremendously enthusiastic about *It Won't be Long Till Christmas* and will be most co-operative. I think you should contact him right away and see if you can set up a TV appearance on some variety show for Anne to sing this song. Also Anne has indicated her willingness to work the provinces as I understand you now can gain some excellent radio air play in the local stations around the UK. We plan to get good radio play over here and would consider bringing Anne over to the States for a spot on *The Tonight Show,* or one of the New York variety shows.

Regards
JAJ"

I am sorry to say I do not know who these men were (other than Tutti) but judging from the letter it would appear it was an American representative from the US based Disney recording studio, to Anne's recording company

To finish this chapter on a personal note, many a trendy outfit was bought for me by my aunts in the 60s on our regular visits to Carnaby Street, London. I was firstly a 'Flower Power' girl, minus the whacky baccy and moved on to be a 'Mod' as opposed to a 'Rocker'

Anne was well and truly keeping up with the times....she loved the whole thing!

Chapter Six

The Changing 70s

With the vast change in music preference, Anne's career was not as it had been. Although she was still loved and very much in demand by the previous generation, her career had taken on a new phase. There were still TV appearances, she mostly appeared in cabaret, but was still being kept very busy. She also donated more of her time to perform in numerous charity shows. This suited Anne, as it gave her more time to spend at home, something she welcomed, having spent many years at the top of her career, living out of a suitcase. She was still an attractive, active woman who was enjoying more free time allowing her to concentrate on the things she loved doing and her hobbies. Although having said that, she had slowed down, compared with the previous decade, but when you take into account the number of appearances she made as either guest artist or panel member between 1969 and 1972 on the BBC alone, maybe there was not such a decrease in work commitment. Here are the following programmes she was featured on during that time.

1969-: Galaxy, Sounds Familiar, Petticoat Line, Open House, Roundabout and the Sam Costa Show.

1970-: The Organist Entertains, Those Were the Days, Sounds Familiar, Twenty Five Years Ago, Sounds Great, Music with Love, Charlie Chester Show, Accent on Melody and Open House.

1971/72-: She appeared with BBC Radio Orchestra in The Light Music Festival at the Royal Festival Hall. Twice on the Tony Brandon Show and was interviewed by Alan Dell on The Golden Age of British Band.

I must say that since her mother's death a slight tension had developed at home between David and Jo. Nothing major mind, but Jo and David often had words. If I am honest, I think David might have been somewhat jealous of the closeness between the two sisters, but that was never going to change. David was a great golfer and spent many a day at the golf club now that he had this newfound freedom from travelling with Anne all over the country, in fact the world. Golf was also a sport that Jo embraced, Anne did try a couple of rounds at the club, but decided it was not for her, she put her poor performance down to the fact her bust was too big and got in the way of her swing!!

Often the sisters would spend time at home alone with each other and enjoyed it greatly. Jo was the only one of the two that could drive and they would take themselves off shopping to Oxford Street or to their hairdressers, *Raymond's of Knightsbridge*.

One of Anne's interests was jewellery; she had a desirable collection. She loved all jewellery especially rings, the bigger the stone and the more it shined the better. Her engagement ring is pictured in this book. It is a 1920s cocktail ring. She had so much and never tired of looking in antique shops, especially in Burlington Arcade, Piccadilly hoping to increase her collection. She preferred old to new. She told the story of when she first met the Queen, she could not take her eyes off a diamond brooch that Her Majesty was wearing, and she almost forgot what they were talking about.

Her other love was history. Her favourite period being Tudor, (must have been all those gems that Elizabeth 1st wore) and Jacobean. She was very knowledgeable and always held me spellbound when she was telling stories from those times. She had a very vivid imagination and could make up an interesting story about pouring a cup of tea!

Anne was also a very good artist, spending many a day with canvas and oils in the garden. She painted me a picture once of a sailing boat at sea, this I still have, along with others.

While we are still on a personal note, I can recall so vividly, how supportive both Patty and Josie were to me through a very traumatic time in my life back in 1972. I had just returned to

England having spent the previous nine months touring the States. I had been travelling with a very close friend of mine and we both found the return to our families hard, having had so much freedom. I had something that I needed to share with my parents, but did not know how. My stay in the States had been cut short, as my mum had suffered a mild stroke. I was worried about her and felt I should be with her. Due to her health scare, I was not sure if it was the right time to tell her my news, as I thought it might upset her. I turned to my elder sister for advice and I must say she was about as useful as a chocolate fireguard! I decided on Boxing Day, to tell my mum that I was gay. She looked horrified and said to me, "do you mean you are a lesbian?" I told her yes, and she burst into tears, and started to ask me where she had gone wrong, and how had she failed me. I felt so awful. I did not know what to do. I phoned Patty and Josie who were at a party at their next-door neighbours. I spoke to Josie and asked if she and Patty could come to us as we had a problem. Josie asked if we needed David to come, I suggested it might be better if he stayed at the party. Within ten minutes they had arrived looking as glamorous as ever. Mum, who was still very upset, told them my news. Their reaction was incredible. Patty said 'Eileen, come on, did you not know that? Jo and I have known Kelly was gay from the age of five (that was a bit before I did I thought) Josie went on to say 'What is the big deal? She is still our Kelly, your baby.' They started to make light of it all and to make mum laugh, as they always could, and after what seemed to be half an hour, but was actually three hours, things were fine. Mum and I had a cuddle; we established I did not need any psychiatric help, and that it was not catching, so all seemed well. I told my dad the following day, and he just said, 'that's alright Dinks (a pet name he had for me) as long as you are happy'. The way Patty reacted was so typical of her, she had no prejudice whatsoever, and was tolerant and supportive of everyone's beliefs and lifestyles. In fact so was Josie. They were both such lovely women, full of love and so caring.

I can honestly say that there was never a problem with my sexuality with any of my family from that day on. I have my doubts that David ever knew, as every so often, even up to his last years, Patty and Jo would occasionally mention this fictional 'Derek' that I was meant to know...hey ho. I have been with my current partner Di for twenty years. Patty, Josie and my mum, met her in 1985, and fell in love with her, and she them. Whenever we went to see Patty in concert, and she sang *Lay Down Your Arms* when she got to the lyric…. 'a girl who loves a soldier is either sad or gay' she would always wink at us, those things are precious to us both.

So as I mentioned earlier Anne's career had slowed down a little, but there was still a lot more to come for her. In the years that followed there were countless reunion concerts recalling all different occasions pertaining to the entertainment of forces during the Second World War. Anne was the special guest star at the vast majority of these. One such reunion was the Glenn Miller Anniversary Concert held on 16th December 1975 at the Royal Albert Hall. The Million Airs was the orchestra that was used to re-create the Glenn Miller Army/Air Force Orchestra. They had a string section and a French horn musician. The orchestra was conducted by Malcolm Lockyer, and the late Alan Dell introduced the programme. The whole show was recorded and released on LP, but unfortunately due to some contractual difficulties Anne's contribution to the show was left out, and needless to say her many fans who saw the show, and bought the LP as a consequence were furious.

The Glenn Miller Tribute show took to the road the following year and Anne was on that extensive tour as the regular guest artist. They first appeared on the 24th February at The Corn Exchange, Bedford (which is where Glenn Miller did many a broadcast from back in 1944) the tour then went on to perform at theatres in the following towns: Gloucester, Wolverhampton, Preston, Bradford, Newcastle-on-Tyne, Manchester, Stoke-on-Trent, Paignton, Wimbledon, London, Brighton, Sheffield, Bournemouth and finishing at Coventry on the 4th April. It must have been very tiring for Anne, as these shows ran continually from 24th February to the 4th April without a break. Taking into account all the travelling during the day then performing nightly she must have been exhausted, but once on stage, it would have never shown, she was such a professional. The Miller Tribute Tour was put together by Tony Wild and Doug Le Vicki, in association with the Glenn Miller Society. As a matter of interest the price for the best seats at these concerts was £4.00. Rather depressing when you think what we pay for a theatre ticket these days, and I would not say the standard of performance is any better, would you?

Still on a remembrance theme, on 4th May 1978 there was another concert held at the Royal Albert Hall to celebrate the 33rd anniversary of the end of the European War which was in aid of the Soldiers, Sailors and Air Forces Association (SSAFA) called *Evening of Nostalgia*. The late Lord Louis Mountbatten and Prince Michael of Kent were the guests of honour. Anne sang twelve songs and the show ended with her singing *Land of Hope and Glory* accompanied by the choir and full orchestra, it was a moving moment. Anne received rapturous applause and indeed, a well deserved standing ovation.

Also in 1978 Anne was invited to perform in a very special show and felt honoured to be asked. This was the *'Royal Variety Performance'* at the London Palladium on the 13th November in front of Her Majesty the Queen Mother.

Anne was still giving much of her support to entertaining the services. She gave two concerts for the Chelsea Pensioners including a Founders Day concert before Prince Charles. Carrying on with a military theme, she also performed in front of an audience made up of ex RAF prisoners of war at the Mermaid Theatre, London. Anne also made a special guest appearance at a POW dinner in London, again in front of Prince Charles. In all Anne appeared in over twenty major charity concerts, as well as a series of shows with the 'Royal Artillery Concert Orchestra', conducted by Captain Stan Patch (RA). One of these shows was held at the Grand Hall in Wembley Conference Centre on the 4th November 1978, and was called *An Evening with Anne Shelton*. The compere for the show was Monty Modlyn. Also on the bill were

Bert Weedon, and comedian Tony Dowling.

In 1979 Lieutenant Colonel Ryder of the U.S. Army organised a 'friendly invasion of Britain' of American forces from the 1939-45 War to revisit the beaches on which they landed on 'D' Day. The response was overwhelming, 1,200 ex-servicemen were taken to Bournemouth where they all celebrated their re-union with all the inhabitants of Bournemouth taking part. The men were asked which artist they would like for the cabaret, without any hesitation they all agreed they wanted Anne Shelton. Anne performed three cabaret shows for them during the week they spent in London and Bournemouth, before they left to re-visit the beaches in Normandy.

About this time, maybe a few years later Anne had a new Musical Director. Again a very talented pianist and arranger called Ronnie Price. Ronnie was more commonly recognised as the pianist featured on *Name That Tune*. He was to stay with Anne for the remainder of her career. We will hear more of Ronnie and Anne's relationship later.

Anne was one of the stars invited to take part in the all woman show from the London Palladium. She also starred in the E.N.S.A. Charity Show held in Salisbury, which just so happened to be the place where E.N.S.A first started during the last war. E.N.S.A by the way stands for Entertainments National Service Association.

The final event that I would like to include in this chapter from the seventies was very important to Anne. In 1979 a film called *Yanks* was released. It was directed by John Schlesinger and the screen writer was Colin Welland. The whole film was mostly built around the well used wartime phrase regarding the U.S troops stationed here, which was 'Over paid, over sexed, and over here'. Filmed in Yorkshire it depicted a time during the Second World War when tiny towns in parts of rural England were dominated (much to some of the young English lads disgust) by thousands of U.S. troops in the run up to the 'D' Day invasions. The story line is that of an American Sergeant (played by Richard Gere) who falls in love with the local shopkeeper's daughter. The interplay between the Yanks, and the Brits is most amusing, and the film was a great box office success.

John Schlesinger approached Anne and asked if she would sing the final song in the film *I'll be Seeing You*. This was a great honour coming from such an acclaimed producer, and of course Anne accepted. She was so elated to think that she, as an English performer, had been chosen over an American to sing out the film, bearing in mind it was an American production.

The premiere of *Yanks* was held in New York and John Schlesinger very much wanted Anne to be there. United Artists, who made the film, invited Anne, Jo and David to attend. In the evening after the premier a grand ball was held. They asked her if she would be prepared to do a cabaret spot singing *Ill be Seeing You,* Anne agreed so they booked the Tom Dorsey band which was conducted by Buddy Morrows. For the band to play at the event they had to be flown in from California. It was apparently a very good night and most deservedly, Anne received yet another standing ovation.

When the premier was held in London the guest of honour was Princess Anne and her then husband Captain Mark Phillips. Anne once again was asked by John Schlesinger to attend. This was another great occasion.

My aunt was very excited about her involvement in Yanks and as usual she had so many interesting stories to tell about her time at the American premier. I must say all through my life, knowing her as well as I did, I can honestly say she never once when relating these amazing stories sang her own praises, she was always in awe of the others present. She most certainly was never full of herself, as sadly so many are today.

Something else happened to Anne in the 70s that I cannot spend too much time on as astonishingly enough nor did she. She married her fiancé of so many years David Reid. It was such a low key event that the only people there were Anne, David and two witnesses. It seemed so out of character for her being such a family person, not to want to share the event, but that is the way she wanted it. I almost felt that after being together for so long it seemed pointless to marry, but they must have had their reasons.

She never used the name Reid, except on her passport, even then it read as Anne Shelton-Reid. She also never discussed the wedding.

Where have the 70s gone? Best move on to the 80s.....

Chapter Seven

The 'Not Forgotten' Association and the 80s

The NFA played a great part in Anne's life in her later years. I feel that my aunt would want me to include the association in her biography.

I am sure many of you reading this will be well acquainted with the NFA, but those of you that are not, please allow me to give you an insight into the good work that they do.

The 'Not Forgotten' Association is a charity for the ex-servicemen disabled from all conflicts. Here follows a little about their history.

In 1919, a year after the Armistice which ended the terrible carnage of the Great War, a lady was visiting her local hospital. She asked the matron if, by chance, she still had any wounded servicemen under treatment. 'Six hundred' came the bleak reply. The lady - Miss Marta Cunningham, a famous singer, was horrified and soon discovered that in fact there were thousands of badly wounded men lying in hospitals up and down the country, bored, lonely and in pain. Miss Cunningham established the The 'Not Forgotten' Association with the object of providing entertainment and recreation for the hopelessly war crippled, giving them anything to alleviate the tedium of their lives and to give them something to which they could look forward.

HRH Princess Mary, later the Princess Royal became the NFA's first patron and remained so for the rest of her life. She was succeeded by HRH The Duchess of Kent who remained patron until 2000.

Sadly there are thousands of disabled ex-servicemenmand women in this country. They have been injured in conflicts around the globe over many decades. Now most of them are elderly and often frail and although their essential needs may be provided for, the NFA is able to give them some of the 'extras' which most of us take for granted, something to look forward to - something to make life worth living. Those eligible are ex-service or serving men and women who have a War Pension or are in receipt of compensation from the Armed Forces Compensation Scheme, or who are currently suffering from some form of ill health. They ensure that these people are not forgotten by providing entertainment in many forms, which brings happiness and joy into their lives. As the years have gone by, the Association has adapted to meet changing needs and extended its activities to include those wounded in more recent conflicts. Last year they provided entertainment to over 9000 people.

Anne's first official involvement with the NFA was back in 1981. The association was looking for a replacement for Miss Wynn who was retiring from the entertainments committee. Richard Baker, the BBC's news presenter, who was aware of the situation, suggested to the chairman of the NFA, John Brunel Cohen that a good replacement might be Anne Shelton. John thought this to be a great idea and asked Richard if he thought Anne would have the time, and more to the point, be interested in such a commitment. Richard contacted Anne on the chairman's behalf. Anne met with John and he asked her if she felt she could take on the task of engaging artists, on a voluntary basis, to give their time to perform in shows held bi-annually for the ex-service personnel. Anne had many show business friends whom she felt would be more than happy to offer their services for such a well deserving cause.

Anne accepted the offer and once it had been cleared by the other members of the NFA committee, was appointed as the new 'Entertainments Officer'. This was not an official title, but one that was kindly installed upon her by John Brunel Cohen. The patron at this time was HRH The Duchess of Kent.

The first show that Anne organised was in July 1981. As mentioned the shows were held twice a year, the first in July and the second in December. Her Majesty the Queen allowed these shows to be held at Buckingham Palace. The summer show was performed from a large marquee in the Palace grounds and the Christmas show was held in the Royal Stables (minus the horses I am happy to say) The first show was a great success, Anne had made several changes to the format of the performance that were greatly appreciated by John Brunel Cohen and other high ranking committee members. She was acclaimed as their heroine. Anne carried on in her role for many years, providing many stars to entertain the well deserving men and women of the NFA.

Today's patron of the NFA is HRH The Princess Royal.

Applications for assistance from the NFA are generally made through The Royal British Legion, SSAFA Forces Help, Combat Stress or the Welfare Service of the Veterans Agency. Should anyone reading this want to contact 'The Not Forgotten' you can do so by contacting -:

The Director
The 'Not Forgotten' Association
4th Floor
2 Grosvenor Gardens
London SW1 0DH   Telephone-: 0207 7730 2400.

> *"To be remembered is pleasing.....*
> *but 'Not Forgotten' is wonderful!*

~*~

Still in the early 80s it was a busy time for Anne, especially with her new commitment. As I mentioned previously Anne had a new musical director and pianist Ronnie Price. He was married to a woman called Jo and they were a lovely couple who became very good friends with Anne and the family. Ronnie's arranging and style of playing suited Anne's sound very well, and probably he gave her the best accompaniment that she'd had since Johnny Franz was in the driving seat, or should I say, on the piano stool.

Still flying around all over the place, Anne went to Toronto, Canada to appear at The World Re-Union of the R.A.F Association. Former Air Crews from all over the world attended. Still in Canada she went to Winnipeg and was guest of honour together with Sarah Churchill for a reunion of Bomber Command. Sarah Churchill was the daughter of Sir Winston Churchill and was an accomplished actress. She died in 1982.

Not only did Anne have a new musical director, but also a new agent, Johnny Mans, of Johnny Mans Production. One of the other stars that he managed was Norman Wisdom. Having met Johnny many times over the years, as dear and as attentive as he was to Anne, I always felt that he was not very pro-active in promoting her, but it seemed to suit her.

The life-long friendship with Tutti Camarata was still going strong. Despite the miles between them, he lived in California and Anne lived in London, they were in frequent contact and spoke on the phone weekly. He was a kind, gentle man. I remember back in 1972 when I was over in the States travelling mostly by Greyhound bus (as that was all my finances would allow being a young student) my friend and I met up with him at his recording studios in Hollywood. He asked how we were planning our trip home and I explained that mostly it would be overland. He then produced from his wallet enough money for my friend and I to fly back to our base in Canada to enable us to catch an earlier flight home. It was such a kind gesture, but that was the sort of man he was. Not only did Anne and Tutti share a love of music, but also shared the same religion, both being devout Catholics

I would like to concentrate for a moment on Tutti's career. He was born in 1913 in New Jersey. His real name was Salvatore Camarata, nicknamed 'Tutti' by the bandleader Jimmy Dorsey. Tutti was truly a jack of all musical trades – instrumentalist, orchestrator, arranger, composer, producer and even record company executive. He started his career at the age of 21 and went on to big and wonderful things. He worked with Dorsey in the 40s. During the war he enlisted, then on his return was hired by Jack Kapp of Decca Records, as a musical director. In 1944 he arranged and orchestrated for a number of Decca's biggest acts, including Bing Crosby, Louis Armstrong, Mary Martin and Billie Holiday.

In 1945 he was sent to work in England by Decca. I imagine this is when he met Anne. He stayed in England for five years.

On his return to the States he linked up with Disney and was very instrumental with the production of *The Jungle Book*. Tutti approached Disney to open up a studio to enable him to work without having to rely on hiring a studio from other firms in L.A. Disney was dismissive of this idea, so in the end Tutti decided to go it alone. He bought an old auto repair shop on Sunset Boulevard in Hollywood, equipped it with several studios and in 1960 opened *Sunset Sound Recorders*. His first customer was Walt Disney. Tutti also did a lot of classical work.

Tutti and Anne worked many times together and it was back in 1982 when Tutti wrote the music to accompany the words to a song that Jo had written. The song was called *Just Look Around*. There is a story behind the lovely words to this song. One summer's day, Anne and Jo were driving in Dulwich Village and they witnessed road rage between two drivers. Jo said, "Why are people so unkind and spiteful to each other, instead of shouting and swearing all the time why don't they appreciate how much beauty there is in the world and take the time to look around and see how lucky we all are just to be here." A few days later Jo wrote a poem about what she had been saying to Anne regarding how lucky we are to live in such a beautiful world. Anne read the words and thought they were lovely, she suggested Jo should get them published. Jo dismissed the suggestion by saying "Oh no, it's not that good."

Sometime later Tutti was over at their home and Anne asked Jo to show him her poem. This she did and when Tutti read it he was very taken and asked Jo if she would allow him to compose a tune for it. This he did, Anne recorded the song and included it on the last album that she ever recorded *Sentimental Journey* which was first released in 1982. Here are the words of this very moving song.

Just look around and you will find
all the wonders He left behind;
He left them all for us to share,
but most of all for those who care.

A winter's day, then follows spring,
or see a new bird on the wing,
to watch the ocean touch the shore,
to see the blossom bloom once more.

So many eyes that never see,
the things He left for you and me
Just look around, Just look around,
Just look around.

He made the strong to help the lame,
though different colours, we're all the same,
He gave his life, he had no doubt,
when we're in need, we seek him out,
He gave his life in so much pain,
he sacrificed but not in vain,
so if you care you're sure to see,
the things he left for you and me,
Just look around.

~*~

Life was much the same for Anne through the 80s with her appearing up and down the country in cabaret and also as the guest artist on several shows. I think she was beginning to tire of all the travelling, but the three of them Anne, Jo and David kept going.

It was lovely to see them take off from home to go to one of Anne's engagements. Often I would be there to witness the departure! Jo always helped Anne get ready. She used to do her hair, help her to choose what she was going to wear, pack her evening gown, makeup, shoes and any other baggage that might be needed. With Anne ready, that left Jo to start to groom herself. David amazed me how he could go from working in the garden in his old overalls, to being suited and booted in minutes. So with Anne and David ready, they would invariably be waiting for poor old Jo who was left to rush around, so as not to make them late, as this would often cause a verbal run-in with David. Jo and David did row and Anne hated it, always the peacemaker. All three ready they would take off in the Bentley. It was rather like watching Royalty leave home. Anne and Jo would be seated in the back, both looking very glamorous with David driving.

~*~

In 1984 my dad died unexpectedly. As always Patty was there for me and it was she who phoned to say that he had passed on. Mum was not coping well with her loss, so without any hesitation her two sisters suggested that she move back into Glendower, the family home. Life had gone full circle; the three sisters were again as they had been forty years ago, all living together.

Patty was travelling down to Eastbourne one July afternoon in 1989 to appear in a show at the Congress Theatre. As usual David was driving. They were at Tunbridge Wells when David lost control of the car and drove into a brick wall. Thank God none of them were seriously injured, but as you can imagine they were very shaken up. What was more upsetting for Patty is that Jo and David had been arguing on the journey down, I am not sure if this was a contributing factor to the accident or not.

Jo phoned our home and luckily Di was there. She told her that they had just had an accident and asked if Di could come to help them and take Patty to the theatre. Our home was in East Sussex, so Di was able to get to them within half an hour. When Di arrived Patty and Jo were still sitting in the back of the car and David was standing on the pavement. The AA were called and David stayed with the car while Di drove Patty and Jo to Eastbourne. Patty was physically shaking, Jo was calm. It was always the way that

Jo would stay in control, as opposed to Patty who became very emotional at times.

They arrived at the Congress in time for her performance. Patty got ready for the show, and 'Anne' took over. Watching her perform you would never have known what had happened earlier. David arrived at the theatre much later. Ronnie Price, who was playing for Anne, went well out of his way after the show to drive them all home. He was a good friend and showed this many times over the coming years.

This was really a turning point in David's health. He was not looking well and was becoming very subdued, showing very little interest in anything. He was starting to stay at home more, stopped playing his beloved golf, just wanting to sit in front of the television.

Jo also was having health problems. She had lost a lot of weight and was having trouble with her stomach. Patty was very worried about them both, and was praying to God, that they would both be ok. She refused to accept that there could be anything major wrong with either of them, as they were both so very important to her and I am sure she could not have envisaged life without them. As a matter of interest Patty had never spent a night or day on her own, throughout her life, she had always had company.

Chapter Eight

The Good And The Bad Times Of The 90s

The year 1990 started well for Anne. David still did not seem to be his normal self, but nothing had been diagnosed from the medical examinations that he had. Jo also had spent much time at the doctors and was due to see a consultant, but again nothing was showing from the blood, and other tests, that she had.

For many years a lot of people had felt that Anne should receive some kind of award for her services to the country, its armed forces and her tireless work for the many charities she supported, such as 'The Not Forgotten'. It was thought unfair that Vera Lynn had been made a Dame, but Anne had nothing. Anne was the sort of person who would never have shown her hurt and disappointment at having been overlooked, but she was deeply hurt.

This was soon to change. It appeared that under the Thatcher government Anne was at last to receive the recognition that she so dearly deserved. In early May she received the following letter from 10 Downing Street.

"Madam,

The Prime Minister has asked me to inform you, in strict confidence, that she has it in mind, on the occasion of the forthcoming list of Birthday Honours, to submit your name to the Queen with a recommendation that Her Majesty may be graciously pleased to approve that you be appointed an Officer of the Order of the British Empire.

Before doing so, the Prime Minister would be glad to be assured that this would be agreeable to you. I should be grateful if you would let me know by completing the enclosed form and sending it to me by return post.

If you agree that your name should go forward and The Queen accepts the Prime Minister's recommendation, the announcement will be made in the Birthday Honours List. You will receive no further communication before the list is published.

I am, Madam
Your obedient Servant

Andrew Turnbull

Anne was so excited when she received the letter. Her name was put forward and it was agreed, and announced in the Birthday Honours List that Anne was now Miss Anne Shelton O.B.E.

Anne did not receive as much publicity as one would have hoped regarding her O.B.E., in fact it was very much overlooked. The late Alan Dell whose programme *The Dance Band Days* was very popular for many years and on which Anne was often featured was extremely critical of the BBC because no mention of her award was made over the air by the Corporation. He could not understand why this was the case, taking into account the association Anne had with the BBC for so many years.He remedied this colossal faux par, as he saw it, by dedicating the whole of one of his programmes to Anne, shortly after she received the O.B.E.

Anne was not to enjoy her new happiness for long, as fate had another blow waiting in the wings. David's health deteriorated rapidly and he died on the 11th June 1990, having suffered a massive stroke. Di and I were in California at the time of his death. Patty decided that she did not want to tell us while we were away and upset our holiday, so they delayed the funeral until our return home. She was always thinking about everyone else even when she was experiencing great sadness.

Like the trooper she was she soldiered on. There were now just the three sisters in the very large house. I did at this time suggest maybe they should move to East Sussex to be near us, but that suggestion was completely ignored.

In July, Anne was getting ready for the summer show at Buckingham Palace for the 'Not Forgotten'. This time the show was to take on a new theme. Instead of the artists performing for the audience from a stage, there was to be a celebrity walkabout during a garden party, which had the Queen and Prince Phillip in attendance. The stars would mingle, and talk with the ex-servicemen and women and refreshments would be served in the marquee. It was a truly great day. Although it was the first time that Anne had not had David there, she did have Jo, Eileen, Di and me there for her. The stars appearing were Bert Weedon, Lorraine Chase, The Beverley Sisters, Elizabeth Welch, Teresa Cahill, June Brown (Dot Cotton from Eastenders) Pam St Clement (Pat Butcher from Eastenders) and Lesley Crowther.

After the show we went back to Dulwich and had fish and chips. It was the happiest I had seen Patty, Josie and mum for a very long time. They all got on so well and were coping admirably on their own without a man around.

Jo was still not feeling well and she was worried as to what was wrong. All the tests she underwent were coming back either negative or inconclusive. I think she knew there was something wrong, but was concerned that they could not find it. I remember one time when we were at Glendower and the sisters wanted to go and visit their parents' and David's graves. Di and I drove them up to Brenchley gardens. Patty, Di and my mum were tending the graves, and Josie was with me. She needed a lot of reassuring that she would be all right, and I must say she was keeping a brave face on for her sisters. I will never forget what she said to me that afternoon. She was sharing her fears with me about her health. Her biggest fear was that it was cancer. She looked at me with tears in her eyes, and said "who will take care of them (looking towards her sisters) if anything happens to me?" I held her hand so tightly, and told her she would be fine please God, and assured her that if anything ever did happen, Di and I would be there for them.

In July 1991 Anne had a show on the Isle of Man. Jo, although really to unwell to go, went with her, as she did not want her to travel alone. Anne appeared in the show and went straight back to the hotel afterwards where Jo had been waiting for her, as she had been far too ill to accompany her to the theatre. The next day they caught the first flight back to London, but Jo was taken ill on the plane and had to be taken off in a wheelchair. They were met at the airport by their regular driver Ray. He was devastated to see what state Jo was in and suggested she be taken straight to hospital. Anne said she thought Jo would be fine if they could just get her home, she was in denial that there could be anything sinister wrong with her baby sister. Ray told Anne that he was sorry he was going to have to take her to get checked, so he drove straight to Kings College Hospital in south east London, only a few miles from their home in Dulwich.

The first I knew of this emergency was when my mum phoned me early Sunday evening to say Jo was not feeling very well and they were doing some checks at the hospital to see what was wrong. I don't know if she was really unaware of the seriousness of the situation or if, as always she was trying to prevent me from worrying. Mum said that she and a family friend who was staying at the house were going to get a taxi to Kings. Di and I were not happy with what we were hearing so we made a dash to London. When we arrived we found Patty, mum and family friend, Doreen waiting in a small room off one of the wards. They had all been crying and Patty especially looked awful. Josie was in theatre undergoing emergency surgery. After a while I saw two surgeons walking towards the room. They spoke to us all and said that Josie was very ill, Patty immediately said, "She isn't going to die is she?" The softly spoken surgeon replied, "Yes, I am afraid she is." I can honestly say that on hearing those words we all went into shock. My mum started to hyperventilate, Patty screamed and collapsed and I just ran out of the room, not knowing what to do or say. Di as always was so strong, stayed calm and took control. One of the surgeons followed me out. He told me that Josie was already dead, but he did not want to break it to my family straight away as he knew how terribly upset they were.

I went back in and broke the news that our darling Josie had passed on. There and then a part of Patty also died. She never was the same again from that moment on. Her heart was broken beyond repair. The date that changed Patty and Anne Shelton's life forever was 22ⁿᵈ July 1991.

We drove them home. It was absolutely horrible to see the pain in these women that I adored, and knowing there was absolutely nothing I could do to help them through the shock and total disbelief that they had lost their Jo.

There is not really a lot more I can say. The funeral was arranged; Josie had a full requiem mass at St Thomas Moore's in Dulwich. I was one of the coffin bearers, as I did not like the idea of only strangers carrying her to her final resting place. She was buried along with David and her brother Bill. Jo's biggest fear was confirmed, she died of cancer. The tumour was hidden by part of her bowel and therefore was not detected.

Later that month Anne still went ahead with the summer show for the NFA. I will never know how she did it. She said that Jo would have wanted her to and the show must go on in memory of her. It was so sad to see the change in her, she really didn't have the desire to go on, but she did for the sake of her remaining sister and me. There were a lot of people who cared for Anne and were there to support her, such as her agent Johnny Mans, her pianist and close friend Ronnie Price and his wife Jo. Tutti Camarata although across the ocean was in constant contact with Anne, as he was very close to Jo and was devastated at the news of her death.

The next part of this chapter might surprise some of the readers but I do hope it does not upset anyone as that would never be my intention.

After my father's death in 1984, I had a strong belief that his spirit was still with me and felt that I needed some evidence of this. So I went for a sitting with a medium at the College of Psychic Studies, (Queensbury Place, Kensington, London) and I was convinced by what was being told to me that my father was indeed in communication with the medium.

I made several visits through the years and was introduced to a man called Arthur Molinary. Arthur has been with the college for over twenty years. He is a highly gifted and extremely popular medium who is always in great demand. He has given readings to a large number of society people as well as many celebrities. Also he was the first medium to be allowed to give readings to 'lifers' in prison.

He has made a series of programmes for Granada called *Contact Molinary* and has been featured in many books. Arthur mainly works by tuning into a person's aura in order to reach the other world for communication.

After my visits to Arthur I have always come away feeling comforted at what he has had to tell me. As Patty was feeling so bad and was not at all at peace, I suggested she might get some comfort by seeing a medium and having a sitting. Patty did believe in life after death, but she was not sure if it was accepted to seek help from such people by the Catholic Church, and she was a devout Catholic. As I said to her, how can the church take offence when they preach about God the Father, God the Son and God the Holy Ghost? I also went on to say, that Jesus rose again from the dead, so why is the belief of life after death wrong?

She decided she wanted to go to the College of Psychic Studies, so I made an appointment for her with Arthur. She wanted me to go with her, this I was happy to do. Here follows Arthur's account of their first meeting.

"I remember her as being a very dignified lady who insisted on calling me Mr Molinary and not Arthur. She sat in a large armchair and was larger than life, elegantly groomed and beautifully dressed, an overwhelming presence, albeit she was sad and somewhat nervous, as she had never been to a medium before. Also apprehensive as she made it quite clear she wanted words of comfort and not sympathy about her family who had passed on. She wanted to know they were free from pain and at peace.

She was a very religious lady and had her own beliefs but respected those of other people. She had always been a big lady but when I saw her she had lost a lot of weight due to her husband's passing and also her sister Jo. Jo was Anne's closet friend and they were a very close family.

Anne was in a disturbed state of mind as the two closest people to her heart had died. She desperately needed to know where they were and how they were. Life without Jo just didn't seem to have any meaning and she needed to know if she was happy wherever she was.

In that first reading Jo came through to Anne and said she was dancing with David, she no longer had pain and was laughing again. She told her sister Anne that the nail varnish she had on her nails was 'not hers' (in actual fact they both wore the same colour but since Jo's death Anne had been using Jo's bottle of nail varnish, and in fact had used it that day.) Lamma, Anne's mother, also came through to Anne and said she was helping her to adjust, as Anne was feeling so empty, lost and alone. Her father Bill was also trying to give support. Jo told Anne that she must carry on working and she would always be with her at the side of the stage just as before. After the reading Anne told Kelly that on several occasions while on stage she had felt Jo's presence. Jo also told Anne she must be strong for Eileen and Kelly."

For those who might be doubtful of this account, I can confirm all that was said, as my aunt had the sitting recorded and I still have the tape.

Although still very lost and sad, Patty did find comfort from her sitting with Arthur.

Just to mention that my mum, Eileen died on the 5th Sept 1996, so all three of my 'Little Guardian Angels' are together, and keeping an eye on me, I am sure

Patty Sibley aged about 8

Baby Jo Sibley

A chubby Jo at 11

Anne's mother, Lamma

Lamma in a saucy pose!

Anne's brother, Bill jnr

Anne's mother was called Mrs
Shelton

Patty, second row extreme left, at convent with a stern priest!

Eileen, second from left, front row.

Anne's sister Eileen on the far right, the only one who did not sing

A young Anne with so much in front of her

Above, pin up girl Anne, and
(left) pretending to smoke,
which she never did!

At home with the Sibleys, or the Sheltons as they had become,
Lamma, Jo, Anne, Bill and Eileen at Glendower.

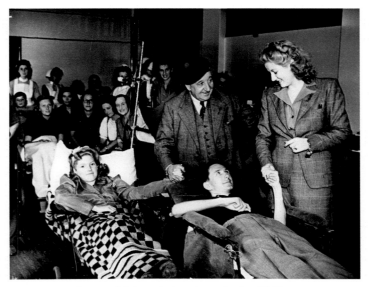

Anne with hospital patients in the 1940s

Anne wearing her 1920's
engagement ring

Anne and Bing Crosby at the
Queensbury Club, London, 1944

Anne with a signed picture from her admirer Sophie Tucker

Cartoon of the crew of HMS Tormentor at Christmas 1943. David Reid is second from the left at the top.

A young Anne meets a young Queen

A very rare picture of Vera Lynn, Anne, David, Eileen and Lamma

Anne's parents at a Masonic function. Bill didn't like formal occasions

Brother in law George Richards (the author's father), sisters Eileen and
Jo and Mr and Mrs Bontoff at a Masonic ladies' evening

Anne and Johnnie Ray, a friendship that blossomed

One of her early visits to America with Percy Faith on her right

Sophie Tucker

Meeting Princess Margaret

Anne with Johnny Franz and a friend

Jo with David and Bill at the height of her career

Anne, Johnnie Ray and Alma Cogan

A very special picture to Anne from the legendary Robert Mitchum.
The inscription reads: "The purity and warmth of your own gift
reawakens in me a faith which shames my own miserly contribution.
Faithfully Bob"

Frankie Laine

Johnnie Ray, a good friend

Phil Silvers

Cesar Romero

Anne gets ready to swing,
look out Chang!

Anne helps Jo to dress, a
reversal of roles

Gracie Fields at the finale of a Royal Command performance. Anne is in
the front line with many familiar faces.

Anne with Prince the corgi

Tossing a pancake!

Slimline Anne

Anne and Jo in the 50s

Anne arriving home, with
"Christmas" the monkey, from the
USA in 1951

Anne (top) and Jo in
Alassio

Jo and Anne on the Norfolk Broads

Frankie Vaughan and Anne.
He sang at her memorial
service in 1994

A swinging Anne

Freddie Mills in training

Sheet music for a great hit

My sister Stephanie, David, me
and Anne holding Ling

A word from Sophie Tucker

All the nice girls love a sailor, and they certainly loved Anne!

Anne and I on holiday in
Middleton-on-Sea with Ling.

Below, that's me again with
Mother St Patty!

Anne in the middle with two real nuns, sister Jo
and the author's sister Stephanie

Anne and Freddie Mills were lifelong friends.
Here he is in training, to the right of Anne.

Anne relaxing at home with her dog Ling

Jo and Anne with the author's sister Stephanie

A day at the races in Perth, Scotland, for Anne, the author and Callum Kennedy

Jo Shelton pours a drink at the bar

Anne with her gold disc from the United Nations, awarded in 1963.Looking on is Yul Brynner.

The Beverley Sisters, who worked with Anne many times over the years.

Anne in a glamorous hat

Rehearsing with
Tutti Camarata

Anne, Jo and the author,
Christmas 1975

An all star line up being presented to the Queen Mother by Bernard Delfont. With Anne are Harry Secombe, Max Bygraves and Arthur Askey.

Prince Charles welcomes Anne to her first show for the Not Forgotten Association

The glamorous side of Anne Shelton

Anne chats with the Duchess of Kent, at that time patron of the Not Forgotten

Talking to Princess Anne with Lonnie Donegan looking on

Ronnie Price and Di at The Palace

The author and Di outside Buckingham Palace. Where is everyone?

Zeke Zarchy, "Peanuts Hucko and Ray McKinley at RAF Larkenheath, Suffolk, in 1984 for a Glenn Miller revival event.

Tutti Camarata, his son, Jo and David. Anne took the picture

Anne with her dear friend Alfred Marks

Anne, Lonnie Donegan and Jo at the Palace

Another great friend, Stanley Black

Chatting with Prince
Charles

With Bert Weedon

With fellow Catholic,
Max Bygraves

Alan Randle, Bert Weedon, Elizabeth Welch, Anne and Ivor Spence

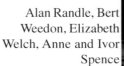

Lorraine Chase, Anne and Mrs Alfred Marks

The Beverley Sisters thrill ex-servicemen at the NFA party in 1990

Prince Philip on walkabout at the Palace show in 1990

HM The Queen escorted by John Brunel Cohen at the same event

June Brown (Dot Cotton), Pam St Clement (Pat Butcher) from Eastenders with Teresa Cahill and Anne

Glendower in Dulwich, London, the family home for 50 years.

Anne's gold disc hanging in the dining room at the Dulwich home

At last Anne proudly shows off her OBE

Anne's concert at The Docklands in 1994, shortly before she died

The very last public performance at HMS Daedalus

Rosemary Squires, one
of the last stars to
appear with Anne

Teresa Cahill, a great
admirer of Anne's work

Original paintings by Peter Miller which were sent to the author

DATED 22nd April 1941.

BERT AMBROSE
— and —
PATRICIA JACQUELINE SIBLEY
— and —
WILLIAM FREDERICK SIBLEY

Agreement

Anne's contract with the
legendary Bert Ambrose
signed in 1941

An Agreement

made the Twenty-Second
day of April One
thousand nine hundred and
forty-one B E T W E E N BERT AMBROSE (hereinafter called
the Manager) of the one part PATRICIA JACQUELINE SIBLEY
(professionally known as Anne Shelton) an infant (hereinafter
called the Artiste) of the second part and WILLIAM FREDERICK
SIBLEY (hereinafter called the Guarantor) of the third part

W H E R E A S the Manager has agreed to act as Manager and
sole agent for the Artiste on the terms and conditions hereinafter
set out —

A N D W H E R E A S the Guarantor has agreed to guaran-
tee the due performance by the Artiste of the terms and conditions
hereof —

H O W IT IS HEREBY A G R E E D as follows :—

1. T H E Manager will at all times during the currency of
the agreement use his best endeavours to further the Artiste's
interest by obtaining for her such engagements (hereinafter
called the said Engagements) on the stage or concert platform
or films or broadcasting or gramophone recordings or all other
engagements which may be to her professional advantage —

2. T H E Manager will at all times during the currency of
this Agreement give or arrange at his expense for all tuition
and training for the Artiste which he in his sole discretion may
consider desirable for her advancement and the Artiste agrees to
attend regularly and punctually all appointments made for such
tuition and training —

3. T H E Artiste appoints the Manager her sole Agent for
the purpose of negotiating the said engagements as are specified
in Clause 1 hereof —

Programme for the 1953
Royal Variety performance

Certificate awarded for
appearing on the Royal
Command performance

Anne's engagement ring
is a diamond, sapphire
and ruby 1920s cocktail
ring.

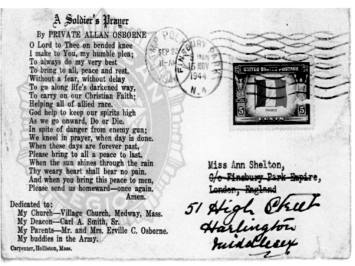

A soldier's prayer sent to Anne in 1944

Anne Shelton, O.B.E.
Golden Anniversary in Show Business

Anne's golden anniversary in show business celebrated at the Berkley Hotel in August 1990

The Berkley Hotel
Sunday, 5ᵗʰ August, 1990

The "Not Forgotten" Association

Founded in 1920 by the late Miss Marta Cunningham, C.B.E.

Patroness: H.R.H. THE PRINCESS ROYAL
Chairman: Group Captain SIR LOUIS GREIG, K.B.E., C.V.O.

Grand Christmas Party

Royal Riding School, Buckingham Palace

Season's Greetings and Best Wishes

"TO ALL DISABLED EX-SERVICE MEN IN HOSPITAL"

THIRTY FIRST YEAR   Thursday, December 6th, 1951

A programme from a 1951 Christmas show at Buckingham Palace, and, below, the billboard at the London Palladium in the 1950s

Chapter Nine

Time to move on.....

Patty and my mum had moved down from Dulwich in February 1994. It was so good to have them near to us, and for us to be able to take care of them, and for me to spend quality time with the two closest people to me, as opposed to having to drive to London to spend a few hours, and then drive back to East Sussex.

I was constantly concerned for their safety and considered them to be very vulnerable as they were two ladies living together in a very large house in very open grounds, backing on to Dulwich Park. They were once broken into several years ago and it had a devastating effect on them all. At that time David and Josie were alive. The thieves had broken in through a downstairs window, and David was awakened to find a man in his room searching through his desk. The man ran off and David was so shaken that he never really recovered from the shock.

They increased security after the break in but I don't think they ever really felt safe there again, and in fact virtually became prisoners in their own home, hardly ever leaving it unattended, even when Patty had to work she would ask a friend over to house sit, as she was so afraid of intruders.

Patty and mum were just muddling through for two years after Josie's death. My aunt and mum were adamant that they would not move. I can understand how they both felt, as Glendower had been the family home for so very long.

The house had witnessed so many memories, mostly happy, some very sad, and I felt the time had come where the happy memories had been outweighed by sadness.

They were both very lonely and were dependant on hired cars

or lifts from friends to get them around, as neither Patty nor Eileen had ever learnt to drive. I lived so very far away that it prevented me from coming up to Dulwich as frequently as I would have liked.

When Jo was alive it was very different. She was the driver and the organiser. She ran the home and the other two sisters were more than happy for Jo to be at the helm. The sisters had so much fun together and enjoyed the simple things in life. Patty and Jo would take off in the car to go shopping usually mid afternoon, as neither were early risers and would return hours later with the supplies. They were all so very happy until Josie died, then their whole way of life just turned around.

Things were getting worse. Mum was virtually house bound as she needed a hip replacement and refused to have it as her fear for hospitals was so great. Patty had all of a sudden become the head cook and bottle washer and was not managing the roll with her usual professionalism!

Di and I visited but both having full time jobs the visits were not as often as we would have liked. We were up in Dulwich visiting Patty for her birthday in November, 1993. I could tell by looking at them that they were not coping well and they seemed to have lost the wonderful sparkle they once had and the laughter seemed to have disappeared. The house and its occupants were sad!

It was very hard for me to watch this happening, as Glendower had once been such a house of fun and merriment. If walls could talk, the stories Glendower could tell. The wonderful Christmases, great New Year parties with such famous faces in attendance. The sunny summers, where I spent so much time playing on the tennis court with Jo, Patty and David. Memories of David tending to his beans in the vegetable patch, and Patty painting a view of the garden, whilst Jo sunbathed. Watching Lady, the Great Dane, chasing the rabbits......and so many more memories.

I decided I would try one more time to get them to agree to move closer to us in East Sussex. Please God, let them see sense.

We had all just finished our meal, and were just chatting, I took hold of Patty's hand and looked straight into her still magical blue eyes, and said to her, "Please my darling Patty, please move down to East Sussex so that Di and I can be closer to you and take care of you properly." I will never forget the look on her face, and the delight in my heart, when she said; "Yes Kelly, the time has come, we cannot manage anymore in this big house on our own."

I was so relieved, but I realised that my work had just begun, and that the sale, and finding a new home for them would not be easy. Little did I know then, the antics to follow.

Patty went into Anne Shelton mode and was not making it easy to sell the house. I think a lot of the problem was her fear. I could understand her concerns. She was planning to move from a house that she had spent nearly fifty years in and leaving London, where she had been all through the war, and had worked so many venues in and around the centre of London. She kept changing her mind as to when she would be ready to move but I realised I had to keep on the case and became a bit bossy!

One thing she said to me on one of her negative days will stay with me until the day I die. I told her that we really must put the house on the market and arrange for it to be valued, she said, "If I move from here I will die." I dismissed the comment as her being silly, but little did I now she would be dead in eight months time. I knew then that I had to act fast before Christmas came, as she might well change her mind and refuse to move.

I contacted Hamptons Estate Agents. They had a very good reputation as vendors for such properties as Glendower. I spoke to a charming agent, whose name I am afraid escapes me, and a date and time was arranged for him to come and carry out a valuation on the house.

Patty had expressed a wish not to be there whilst the agent was carrying out his valuation, so Di agreed to take her shopping, and not to return until the 'intruder', as Patty thought of him, had gone. My mum was happy to stay, as I think she was more enthusiastic to move than her younger sister.

The house was valued at a very high figure, an amount that I think shocked Patty. As a matter of interest, she paid £5,000 for the property back in the 40s. I instructed Hamptons to place Glendower on the market and the agent told me that he felt there would be great interest. It was decided that there would not be a 'For Sale' sign put up, as was my aunt's wish.

It was very apparent that Patty was not going to have anything to do with buying or selling of homes. She decided that she wanted to hand all the responsibility over to me. You must remember that despite all her success in her professional life, she had always had a manager, or agent there for her to take care of her affairs but when she was about to embark on the biggest change in her life, she could not face it without support. I contacted my solicitor and he arranged for me to have power of attorney. This gave Patty the support she needed, and she trusted me and knew that it would all be all right. It just goes to show how much trust, faith and love we had for each other.

The agent for Hamptons was correct. The interest that was shown in Glendower was quite staggering! We hit upon another slight problem. As you may well understand, this whole ordeal was proving to be very traumatic for Patty. Deep down she did not want to sell her home, but realised that she really did not have an option, as it was becoming very difficult for her to handle my mum's disability, but her heart wanted to stay put, so the move was very much, as it should have been, on her terms.

The idea of having strangers looking around her home over several weeks did not appeal to her at all. I must confess that I found this scenario daunting, as I wanted to be present when any prospective buyer viewed and the idea of shooting up the A21 every other day did not appeal to me at all, working full time it would have proved most problematic. The list of those interested was growing and the chap from Hamptons (I really must try and find out his name, as he emerges as somewhat of a hero at the end of this tale) came up with the great idea of having an 'open day' and booking half hourly appointments, for all those wanting to view on just one chosen day. Go for it!

Again, I am sorry to say, that due to the old brain cells dying off, I cannot remember the exact date, but it was in November

1993. The day dawned when 142 Court Lane, Dulwich, London was open to view.

Di and I arrived early that bright, autumn morning. We were prepared for a hard day ahead. When we arrived, Patty and my mum were ready to be taken to friends who lived locally to spend the day, as neither of them wanted to be present when the prospective buyers came to view. I waved them goodbye, shut the door, and stood in the hall way of this magical house. It was so quiet…really rather eerie. All I could hear was the ticking of the grandfather clock. I looked at the stairs and half expected to see David running down them two at a time, in a hurry, as he was late for a golf match, or Patty walking steadily down carrying a tray with cup, plate and newspaper, having been treated to breakfast in bed after a late night, as she had been in a show the night before. Or my Nan standing at the bottom of the stairs in her pinny shouting up to her two daughters saying, "Pat, Jo are you going to stay in bed all day?" All of a sudden it became very sad for me and I wondered if I was doing the right thing, or should I move to London and let Patty and my mum stay put in their home? Before I had time to ponder there was a knock at the door. I jumped so high, I nearly touched the ceiling but landed soundly on my feet to realise the show must go on!

It was our dear nameless friend from the estate agents. The first viewing was at 10.00 and the last was at 4.00. In all there were twelve couples who had shown an interest in the house. They came and went and Di and I were available to meet them all and to answer any questions.

The day seemed endless, I must say we were both getting rather hungry and hoped the last couple to arrive would come and go as quickly as possible.

The last viewing was in the name of Dr Prescott. The couple arrived before the last couple had left, so I met them and made the classic mistake of addressing the male as Dr Prescott. I felt such a fool when the lady informed me she was Dr P……It transpired that the previous year, this couple had shown an interest in Glendower, and had written to my aunt asking her to let them know should she ever wish to sell. I later mentioned this to Patty, it was indeed the case, but she had dismissed the idea, as I would have imagined she would have.

Dr and Mr Prescott seemed very interested in the house. They stayed well over the allotted half an hour and my stomach was most surely being the guide to tell me it was time they left. I was very aware that Patty and mum were no doubt anxious and wanted to get home. Eventually the house was empty except for me and Di, and our Mr X from Hamptons. Mr X mentioned that the Prescotts, he felt were prospective buyers, along with another couple. So we thanked him for his help, and he left. Di went to collect Patty and mum, with strict instructions to come home with fish and chips and pickled onions.

I was once again alone in the house. Lucky, the cat had decided it was safe to come out from her basket, and was busy purring around my feet asking me for her dinner. I went into the kitchen, poured a glass of wine, sat in the breakfast room and thought...what a day! Things were about to change and Glendower would never be the same again! The house was so quiet and my mind was in a whirl. So much had happened and I must say I had not enjoyed having strangers in my childhood home, and even I was beginning to feel resentful at the idea of the lovely old house belonging to someone else.

Di arrived home with Patty and mum, and thankfully an armful of fish and chips. We all sat down in the breakfast room and got stuck into to the eagerly awaited supper. So many meals had been shared around that table, and I must say this meal felt a bit like the Last Supper! We talked about the day and Patty did not show too much enthusiasm. They both looked so very tired. So Di and I made sure the windows, doors etc were all secured and bade them good night.

The next morning, I had a call at work from our lovely Mr X from Hamptons. As he had predicted there had been two interested parties, one of which were the Prescotts. I knew there was no point in discussing this with Patty, so I phoned Di. It appeared that Dr and Mr Prescott were in a better position to make a swift exchange, and they were offering the full price, so we decided to except their offer.....scary times..Glendower was going, going, gone!!

Now the time had come for Patty and mum to come and view the house that we had already earmarked for them at Stunts Green, near Herstmonceux, East Sussex. It was beautiful and was able to accommodate the furniture and possessions that would be coming down from Dulwich. It also had a large garden, which would give them space to sit and read outside, as they both loved to do, but could be managed with a few hours from a gardener and Di and I, or should I say mostly Di!

We drove to London, picked our two darlings up and travelled back to East Sussex for them to view their, hopefully, future home. The house was in an ideal location. A detached four bed roomed house, with much character, mature gardens back and front and was not overlooked at all. The property was only about half a mile from us, which would enable us to make daily visits. The other bonus was that it was empty...no chain, so once we exchanged we could move in whenever it suited us.

The owner of the property at Stunts Green was a charming gentleman called Bob Macey. I explained our situation and he was most accommodating to our needs. When Di and I first viewed the house we explained to Mr Macey how my mother and aunt would be living there alone and how we felt sure they would be in a position to exchange very shortly.

We arrived mid afternoon one day in November. Patty and mum spent about half an hour looking over the house. I should at this point explain that Patty had not come to terms with the loss of David, or even more so Josie. In fact their rooms in Dulwich had remained virtually as they had left them. This, I have learnt, is common in some cases of bereavement when the bereaved cannot bear to accept that their loved ones have gone. Both deaths had been so sudden that Patty still could not accept it.

Bob Macey accompanied us around the house. When we were looking at the bedrooms, Bob looked a little surprised to hear Patty say, "This can be Jo's room and the one opposite can be David's."

Later on, before we left, Bob took me to one side and said, "I thought you said it was just going to be your mother and aunt who would be living here?" I must admit I did chuckle to myself, when I saw his face after I replied, "It is just them, the other two are dead." But on a serious note, Patty wanted those rooms to hold some of her loved ones personal effects, as she wanted so much to keep their memory alive.

Patty and mum decided that the house was close enough to us for them to feel safe and would suit their needs. So that afternoon we confirmed to Bob Macey that we would buy the house. Patty had already decided she wanted to rename Stunts House, (the new property) Glendower. This we did, and in fact took the original nameplate from Dulwich, and the old Glendower reverted back to 142 Court Lane.

Patty being such a London Gal, found it quite disgusting to think that there was a cesspit in her garden at the new property….her intention was to go on to main drainage as soon as she arrived. "You can take a girl out of London but you can't take the Londoner out of the girl." as my grandmother used to say, and Patty and Eileen were most surely Londoners, but I had great hopes that they would soon enjoy the benefits of living in the countryside.

Events seemed to progress well. After the surveys were completed on both properties, which came back favourably and a return visit from the Prescotts to Dulwich with their builder, a date was set for exchange of contracts. It was to be the 8th December. Patty was happy with this date. She saw it as a good omen, as that date would have been Josie's birthday. The completion date was most certainly not to be before Christmas, as this would not have suited either party. So what with Christmas looming and numerous other factors, a completion date was set for 8th February 1994.

Christmas came and went, and February came around very quickly, all too quickly for Patty I am sure. She was so sad about leaving her home that she had lived in for over fifty years, and in fact I was really beginning to wonder if I had done the right thing.

I was sad, so I can imagine how she felt.

We wanted to make this major upheaval as easy as possible for our two dearest ladies. We made it clear to them that they did not have to worry about a thing, we would do it all. The plan was that the Friday before the move, we would drive mum and Patty down to our house, so they would not have to worry about any of the packing or moving. All they would need is a few clothes and toiletries and we would do the rest. This they went along with. The only thing that upset Patty was the fact that Lucky the cat, had to be moved to a cattery for a week whilst the moves took place. She dearly loved Lucky, and was most tearful at the thought, but we took Lucky to a cattery near to us, and Patty was able to visit her through the week should she want to.

Friday 4th February. We arrived early. Both Patty and mum were up and having breakfast. I was so worried how it would go. I felt so much for them both, Patty more than mum, as mum had only moved back to Glendower after my father's death in 1984, she had lived elsewhere, for Patty 142 had been home for so long, and that day she would be walking away from all the happiness she had experienced there forever.

Di, was as usual a rock. When the time came for us to leave she just said, "Ok girls time to go." We loaded the cars with the suitcases and Lucky the cat in her new basket. Eileen went with Di and Patty was travelling with me. She put her coat on, took her handbag and went through the front door. She was holding my hand very tightly and she did not look back once. No tears, just a very heavy heart. Right then Patty was Anne Shelton and was handling this traumatic experience with her usual professionalism, it was the only way she could cope.

We arrived back home in Cowbeech about lunchtime. The journey was good with just a couple of stops, as Patty had insisted on checking Lucky was all right. I prepared lunch and settled them both into their room. Patty and mum both looked happy, which really pleased us. I was amazed they were so calm and settled. Thank you God!

A cunning plan was now afoot. To this day, I do not know how my dearest ladies thought that Di and I were going to manage to pack and clear that very large house on our own over the weekend, and they were not aware of the plan that we had.

Several weeks earlier, we had approached our best friends, and asked how they fancied being part of history, in helping us to sort through years of memorabilia and pack up the contents of the house, ready for Pickfords arrival on the 8th. Thankfully they all said they would. I really do not know how we would have managed without them. Patty was not aware what we were up to as she would not have liked the idea of strangers (as they were to her) going through the contents of her home, but we did not have any other option, as it would have been physically impossible for us to do it alone.

Saturday morning was D Day for our little troop of helpers. There were nine of us in total. We travelled in convoy to 142. I can still see our friends' faces when Di and I showed them around the house, and they saw how much there was to do!! Good job they were so far away from home, as they might have changed their minds. We were working in teams of two and I was the supervisor, saying yes or no, to things that could be thrown, burnt or packed. We all worked so hard, and the crates that had been left by Pickfords were being filled and labelled ready for the big move.

At about nine o'clock that evening, I blew the whistle to announce time to stop and eat. I had already decided that I would treat the gang to a curry. So off I went, shortly to return with curry for all. After eating, drinking and a chat, we all went to bed. It must have been the first time in many years that all the bedrooms had been slept in.

Sunday morning we were up early and off to work again. Di had lit a bonfire to burn some of the stuff that would not be going on. I have never seen such a large bonfire in my life. She lit it on the tennis court and I am so surprised that the fire brigade were not called by the neighbours, especially when the unwanted golf balls that a friend had thrown on the fire started to explode shooting off in various directions!

It might seem harsh to some readers that I had decided to burn or throw away certain things, but I had to, as my family had all been great hoarders and the new house was just not big enough to take everything.

Early Sunday evening we were all exhausted and it was time to go back to East Sussex, as all our friends had work on Monday. There was still a lot to do and this would now be down to me and Di to try and complete the following day.

We worked like Trojans and we thankfully managed to get the house cleaned and contents ready for off. My aunt had paid a phenomenal amount to have Pickfords Removals, as she wanted to make sure all arrived in East Sussex, safe and sound. Sadly it turned out not to be the best choice. The removal day dawned. Before I had time to sit and reflect on the passing of the house, the two lorries arrived and eight chaps were walking down the drive. They all went their separate ways and before I could say Lucky's whiskers, they were on the move. It did not bode well when the first thing I observed was a plant pot being dropped. Thankfully, it was not of any financial value, but of sentimental, as a lot of belongings coming to Sussex were.

Next little problem, a call from the master bedroom (in fact the room which I was born in) "We 'ave a problem up 'ere lady."

What a surprise I thought. I went upstairs to find Mr Jobsworth looking at the oak wardrobes shaking his head.

"You say there is a problem?" I asked.

"Yeah your wardrobes ain't gonna fit through the doors, ya gonna aft to pay for a carpenter to come and dismantle em."

"But surely," I responded, "They have not grown since the chap from Pickfords came to estimate the cost of the removal? Would he not have measured to check that the furniture could be removed from the room?"

To cut a very long story short, a carpenter did have to be called to dismantle the wardrobes, and was employed to attend the new house the next day to reassemble, but, the good news was we did not have to pay, as after 'words' with Pickfords management they admitted to the problem being their error. It was later confirmed by my aunt that she had had the wardrobes built in the room, probably never thinking she would ever move.

The house that had seemed so full in the morning, by lunchtime was almost empty. The men had gone off for lunch, once again leaving me alone in the house with my thoughts. I was just wandering around, checking all was in order, and that there was no major catastrophe looming. I walked into the hall and saw a man coming down the main staircase, who I most certainly did not recognise. I noticed he was holding a small statue in his hand. " Can I help you?" I said.

"This is Anne Shelton's house isn't it? I am so sorry, but I saw the door was open, and it is obvious that Miss Shelton is moving, and when I saw the men leave I thought the house was empty, and I just wanted a souvenir of her, as I have been a fan of hers for over forty years."

Although I thought the old chap had a bit of a nerve and knew what he was doing was wrong, I could not help but feel a bit sorry for him. I said that if he waited outside I would give him a memento to remember Anne, but I would rather like the statue back. He gave me back the statue of St Anthony and I gave him a signed photograph. The old chap seemed very embarrassed, but was also pleased with his memento. I was really shocked to think that an intruder could enter the house so easily, and was pleased that my darlings were out of London and now safe in East Sussex.

The move was complete and I met the estate agent at 142 to surrender the keys. The lorries had left, and it was now dark. The one last favour I asked of the agent was, would he be kind enough to return my mum's library books to Dulwich Library, this he said he would do. I left him to lock the door and my last memory of 142 was an empty dark house, which I had never seen before, as there was always a welcoming light shinning from the front hall window....bye, bye Glendower, hope you will have happy times again.

The furniture was to stay on the lorries overnight to arrive at Stunts Green the following day....well that was the plan and surprisingly it did!

The news that a celebrity was moving into the village had soon spread, and there were numerous neighbours hovering and paying an unusual amount of attention to their front gardens for the time of year.

The move in went well. We tried our best to make the new Glendower, a smaller replica of the original. This we did to the best of our ability. Patty and mum were still safe and snug at our home, and we had no intention of them moving into Stunts Green until it was completely finished and just as it should be. Beds made up, rooms sorted with all their personal bits as they were in Dulwich, even down to bedside books and glasses at the ready! We could do no more.

It was Friday before the house was complete. We thought it was best for Patty and mum to move in at the weekend so that we could spend time with them there before we both had to return to work on the Monday. I knew it would not be easy, but the time had to come when they had to move out from our home. We arranged to collect Lucky cat, and had planned for her to be there to greet them. It was most fortunate that the décor of the house was to their liking, this made life so much easier, as there were no immediate changes to be made.

Saturday morning had arrived. Di went off to collect Lucky, and planned to take her to the new home and stay with her there until I arrived with my two ladies. We had visited Sainsburys and stocked the fridge and cupboards with all their favourite goodies, including my aunt's favourite tipple, Cream Soda.

I suggested to Patty and mum that it was time to go to Glendower Junior. Patty for the first time shed a tear and said she did not want to leave us, or mostly I think our two dogs. She had become so close to Millie and Beanie, as they had to her.

We arrived at the new house, and it was so lovely for them to see Di open the door into the mini Dulwich! Lucky was so pleased to see them both and was wrapping herself around their legs and reminding them that they owed her at least seven days dinner! Again this caused both Patty and mum to shed a tear.

I think they were very pleased with what we had done. I must say it was home from home!

We cooked Patty's favourite Spaghetti Bolognaise and they both seemed settled. We stayed until late and waited until they were both ready for bed.

I do believe that Patty felt as happy as she could. They both seemed to settle into the new environment, very well. We were constant visitors and had entertaining evenings twice a week, when we cooked a special meal, played music, talked about the old days and laughed a lot! A routine was soon established. They engaged the services of a local lady to keep house for them, also a gardener and a nurse, as mum still needed help daily. I truly believe they both really loved all the company. Life seemed good and the time together was special.

Whilst she was living in East Sussex she became a local celebrity again and I believe this gave her a bit of a lift, as once an entertainer always an entertainer. This newfound recognition did please her, not that she would ever say so. I remember once we took Patty and mum to a fish restaurant at Pevensey Bay called 'The Moorings'. During our meal a woman on the opposite table kept looking at Patty and smiling. My mum noticing this said "what's she looking at?" (not very tolerant of strangers mum, as she got older) Patty said "Oh Eileen don't be so horrible." Shortly afterwards the lady came over and said, "Excuse me, aren't you Anne Shelton?" My aunt smiled with such warmth, it was obvious that it really made her feel good to know she was still recognised, she responded in her usual polite way and they chatted for a little while. Patty always had a way of making everyone feel special this was no exception

June 1994 being the 50th anniversary of 'D' Day, kept Patty very busy thankfully, as she needed to keep as active as she could especially now that she lived in the country and was so far away from the liveliness that she had been used to in London, we did not want her to become melancholy, or more sorrowful than she was already.

She performed in shows at the Docklands in London, an open air performance at Haywards Heath, and also just a few weeks before she died she was the guest artist in a concert at H.M.S. Daedalus, Portsmouth, where incidentally, she had performed exactly fifty years earlier. Di and I accompanied Patty to these engagements and I was the chosen person that took over the role of manager, dresser and general support to her, as had her mother, David and Josie before me.

These shows were in close proximity to each other and Patty found them very tiring. Especially the last show at H.M.S, Daedalus, she performed for nearly two hours and was almost at the point of collapse when she came off stage, she was exhausted.

It was so sad to see, Patty had aged so much since the death of Jo. Both Di and I were very worried about her, neither of us realised just how little time we had left together. Patty was so tired of life, and I even think she tired of being Anne Shelton. One thing I will always be grateful for, is that she was performing and still receiving standing ovations up until the very end.

Chapter Ten

The Night Heaven Gained a Star

This will be the saddest chapter for me to write, as the night that I lost my Patty was one of the worst times in my life.

The week leading up to her death had been very hot. She never really enjoyed the heat and always stayed in the shade as opposed to Jo who was a sun worshiper. I remember that she was hoping the weather would become more favourable for those of us that prefer a cooler temperature, as she had a show on the Wednesday and hoped it would not be a scorcher.

On the Monday she phoned me at work asking me if I could buy a couple of fans, she thought it would be a good idea for her to be cool whilst putting on her makeup on the day of the show. She was very well organised, very experienced and knew all the pitfalls of applying stage makeup, especially when it is very warm.

I dropped the fans off on the way home, she seemed very tired and was intending to have an early night, which was very rare for her, as she was most certainly a night bird. It was nothing for her to stay up until 3am, usually pottering around and listening to Radio Luxemburg, a station you may remember from years ago!

The day arrived. July 27th 1994. We were off to London for the summer 'Not Forgotten' Association show at Buckingham Palace. That year there was a train strike so Patty was very concerned that there would be so much extra traffic on the road, that she wanted to leave very early, she was such a professional, but unlike some today she did not like the idea of being late for anything. We had to be at the Palace for rehearsals at ten. Normally it would be an hour and a half journey from East Sussex to the centre of London, but we left at 6am, allowing four hours for the trip.

We set off, Patty and mum were in the back and Di drove with me riding shotgun in the front passenger seat. Surprisingly the journey went well without too much delay, in fact we arrived at the Palace just before 8.30 am. It was very early, I don't even think the Corgis were awake! But we were there. We were met by Peggy Giles who at that time was with the NFA, and was the NFA representative who made sure Patty had all she needed. I guess this is where I start reverting to 'Anne' as my beloved aunt is now in professional mode....

It was very warm. They had managed to set up fans in the dressing room, which were shared by the other female artists. Something I will share with you that you might find amusing, or shocking, is that in both dressing rooms, behind a screen, the palace provided sand buckets for the artists to urinate in should they need to whilst the show was in progress, as the toilets were a long way from back stage, or back marquee as it was.

Anne was ready for off. She had the order of performance and time allocation for each act, so we went to the rehearsal. I am sure there was no need for her to rehearse but she always did. Ronnie Price her close friend and musical director was ready at the piano, as was her bass player, and again close family friend Jo Mudele, and ready with the sticks at the drums was Bobby Worth.

Anne always performed at least one song at the NFA concerts, but often there was a demand for her to do more, but she never over ran her time allotment, unlike some. She was such a quick witted, amusing lady with a wonderful sense of humour. I remember well, she was singing *Lilli Marlene* at the rehearsal and she changed the lyric somewhat to fit in with her morning's activities. I am not sure if you the reader are familiar with the lyrics of *Lilli Marlene*, but the song goes "Underneath the lamppost by the barrack gate, darling I remember the way you used to wait..." Well, as she was rehearsing she sang; "Underneath the lamppost by the Palace gate, I've been standing waiting since nearly half past eight." It was so like her to be so witty.

We had the luncheon, which was provided by the NFA for the artists. Anne hardly eat anything, how very tired she looked, all this I had put down to the heat.

The show went well. The guests were Bobby Crush, Joe Goodman, Faith Brown, Ray Alan (with Lord Charles) and Frankie Vaughan.

The master of ceremonies, as always was a very charming man called Ivor Spencer, who at the end of the show thanked Anne for her endless effort and contribution to the NFA, as did Sir Christopher Airey.

Anne had been very active and spent a long time chatting at the tables of the veterans at the garden party, most remembered her for her war days. Thankfully it was time for home. Anne returned to being my Patty, I was so concerned for her as she looked so worn out and could hardly keep her eyes open on the way home. I sat in the back of the car with her. She seemed so breathless, this I again put down to exhaustion and heat, unaware of any other problem that she obviously had.

We stopped at Elmers End to buy fish and chips, as I knew both mum and Patty were, or at least should be hungry, but Patty could not stay awake long enough to eat them. We arrived back at Glendower, and we made sure the ladies were settled, Patty went straight to bed.

The next day, Thursday, I decided that I would phone her doctor, as I was worried that she might not be well. Knowing that she would be against any doctor's visit I thought it best to run this by her. Patty agreed to go to the doctors to have a check up, but said she wanted to wait until after the weekend. This I stupidly agreed to. I was heavily committed to work that weekend and, although in contact by phone, did not manage to get to see them. Di, also was working the weekend so the ladies were on their own.

Saturday the 30th July. That night there was the most awful thunderstorm, and electricity supply had failed at Stunts Green. Patty phoned me at work to say the power had gone, and how she was worried and did not like to be in the dark. She was very tearful, but as I was the only manager at the store, I could not leave to go to her. I phoned Di who went up to the house and clambered over numerous boxes in the garage to reach the trip switch and regained the power, albeit restored to a very low voltage. I phoned Patty and suggested she go to bed, and not to worry, it would be all right in the morning, I told her that Di would pop in to drop off her groceries, as usual on the Sunday morning. Patty calmed down and said to me "God Bless you my Kelly, I do love you", and I told her that I loved her very much too.

On my way home from work I drove past their house, but as it was rather late, I thought it best not to call in, as I knew they were both in bed, hopefully asleep.

Sunday was a most glorious morning. It was hard to believe what a storm we'd had the night before. I left for work and, as planned Di was going to drop off the weeks groceries at Glendower on her way to work.

I had a phone call that morning at the store that would change my life forever. It was from the nurse who went to the house daily to tend to my mum by helping her get up and to dress. The nurse said, "Kelly, can you come home, I think your aunt is dead."

I froze and said, "What do you mean you think she is dead?"

The poor woman was obviously traumatised, she went on to say "She is so cold and I cannot wake her up, she has no pulse."

I could not take in what she was saying, my heart started to race and I felt sick. Then I heard my mum, who was on the extension of the phone say, "Oh God no, not Pat dead!" I was in such a state. I told the nurse to go and stay with mum and then told mum not to worry that I was on my way home and everything would be alright.....would it?

My mind was racing. I was in charge of a mega superstore and could not just run out, as I wanted to. My first thought was to get hold of Di. I paged her and related the story. She as always proved to be my rock, she said that she would leave work and go straight to Patty's. Then I phoned a very close friend of ours Jayne Joliffe and told her what had happened, asking her to meet

Di at Glendower, as I knew Di would need help with mum.

I then phoned another member of management who was on leave and told him the situation, I will never forget how wonderful he was. He came straight in to cover for me and also arranged for his wife to drive me home, as he felt I was unable to drive myself.

On the way to Stunts Green from Hastings I was so frightened as to what I was going to encounter, I just did not want the journey to end, as I was so unwilling to accept that Patty was dead, "She can't be, she cannot have left me...

I arrived at Glendower to discover a police car in the drive. To this day I'm not sure who phoned the police, I imagine it was the nurse, and now I realise that a sudden death always requires police attendance.

I was met by Jayne who was holding a red rose in her hand that she had picked from the garden for me, thinking I might want to take it to Patty. Roses were Patty's favourite flower, as well as Lilly of the Valley. I went through the front door and could hardly hear what was being said to me as my heart was beating so loudly in my ears. Di was up in the bedroom with Patty's body, not wanting to leave her until I was home, and wanting to be there when I entered the room. I first went into the lounge where my mum was with the nurse. I will never forget her little face, she was so scared and was crying so deeply...I just took her in my arms, we both sobbed, and I assured her that she would be coming home with Di and me and that she must not worry, we would take care of her.

The house seemed to be full of so many people, it was like a foggy haze. I went upstairs and walked along the corridor towards Patty's room. It was so quiet and each step seemed to take an age. When I arrived at the door of the bedroom, it was ajar, I pushed it open...so scared as to what I would see. Di met me, we hugged, we both were tearful. I turned to the bed where Patty was. She looked as if she was asleep, so peaceful, it was hard to believe that she was dead.

She was lying on her side, with her hand up to her face, clutching a tissue. It seemed so fitting, as a child I called her the 'tissue lady', as she always had a bag full. She just looked so perfect, I thought that if I kissed her on her cheek, as I had done so many times when she was asleep, that she would wake up and give me that wonderful sleepy smile and say, "Hello my Kelly". I kissed her, she did not wake up. I placed the rose in her hand, and told her I loved her.

By this time, Jayne had come up to say that the undertakers had arrived. I hated the idea of her going somewhere strange. The family had always used the same undertakers for years. A firm called Uden's who were based in Dulwich, London. I knew that they would be the firm that would be handling the funeral, but as I was told by Di, it would have to be a local firm that had the initial job of removing her body.... "Oh my Patty, I miss you so much already."

I could not be present when they took her away. God bless them, Di and Jayne oversaw this. I went into the garden, and just realised how my life would never be the same again. I was standing in the orchard and two white butterflies were fluttering just in front of me, and I thought, "Yes, Patty and Josie are now together again."

After Patty had been taken away, I knew it was time to take mum away from Glendower, for good! Di made sure that mum had all she needed for a few days, so that we did not have to return too soon and we headed home.

Jayne had come back with us and proved invaluable throughout the evening. I had no idea how much media interest there would be.

The first people that I phoned were Patty's very good friends Tessa Cahill and Robert Saxton. I then contacted her agent Johnnie Mans. All three were in a state of disbelief, as were we all. Can you tell me, why so many people, when you tell them bad news say; "You are joking?" I must admit this is something I have been guilty of myself, I think it is a nervous reaction.

By about midday the phone just did not stop ringing. I believe that Johnnie had alerted the press and there was a tremendous response from the media due to the fact that this legend and lady of song had passed away. Several stars who appeared with her at the Palace show earlier in the week also phoned, it was very touching.

I spoke to so many people from the press and the BBC. It was so amazing that so many were ready to pay tribute to this wonderful woman.

Friends started to arrive with flowers and offers of support. Johnnie arrived from London, as did Tessa and Robert. By late afternoon there was a large gathering. Jayne had been good enough to prepare some food for us all and we ate and drank to the memory of Patty also known by millions as the one and only *Anne Shelton*.

I really do not know what time everyone left. I remember awaking in the early hours having dreamt that Patty had died and then having the awful realisation that she had.

The next day I was up very early. I could not wait for 9am to arrive so that I could phone Udens to arrange for Patty's body to be collected from Eastbourne mortuary and taken home to Dulwich for the last time.

The death certificate translated to layman's terms stated that she had a massive heart attack. A heart that was so full of love for all had just given out. I was so pleased that she went the way she had. It was a shock for all that loved her, but she did not suffer, and was singing up until three days before she died.

All the arrangements had been made and her funeral was going to be 15th August. Mum and I had decided to delay the date to enable Ronnie Price and his wife Jo to return home to be able to attend the funeral. They were on holiday abroad and probably unaware of her death, which would be a great shock to them as they were very close and very good friends, as well as Ronnie being her musical director.

I had wanted Patty to be buried in the attire that she had spent so many years looking so glamorous in, in other words her stage wear. I chose the blue sequined evening dress that she had worn at the last concert that she had performed for the D Day celebration at Portsmouth earlier in June.

Di and I went to say farewell to her at Udens. Mum decided she did not want to come as she would have found it too upsetting. Even in the coffin she looked ever the star. Patty had requested several items of jewellery be buried with her and this we did. Her nails were immaculate, her hair styled with that well-known kiss curl over her forehead. I sprayed some of her favourite perfume Jean Patou's *Joy* on her, and I felt my Patty was ready for her last performance, one that she said she would never be late for...her own funeral.

My mum had requested that the funeral cortège leave from their old home 142 Court Lane, this we did. It felt so strange standing outside the house, as a stranger on the pavement. A stranger to the house I was born and grew up in, waiting for Patty to arrive, something I used to do so many times as a child when she had been out at a broadcast or whatever, but this time it would not be a welcome home but a sad goodbye.

The funeral cars arrived. Patty's coffin was covered in the most beautiful floral tributes, she was going to make a grand exit...as she should.

The requiem mass was held at her local Catholic church in Dulwich and the priest who conducted the mass was Father John from the Church of The Catholic Actors Guild, Covent Garden, who went on to play an even more significant part in her final farewell.

It was so moving. Her coffin came into the sound of Faure's *In Paradisium*, and after the mass, was taken out to her singing *I'll be Seeing You* a very moving moment. The procession then left for her final resting place, the family grave at Brenchley Gardens. Already buried there were my Uncle Bill, David and her sister Josie

I felt great relief that, as a Catholic, my belief was that it was only her shell that was being put into the ground and her spirit and soul were far away in heaven with her family, where by now she was probably singing to the angels. The funeral was very well attended. There were many people there, but I must say, I was mostly concentrating on the well-being of mum and keeping myself together.

We had her wake (now, there's a good old Irish term for a farewell drink to celebrate a soul having passed on) at Dulwich and Sydenham Golf Club, which was my Uncle David's club and also a venue that we had many a happy 'do' at including my 21st

I went straight to the bar, asking for a large whiskey… I had palpitations and thought the Scotch might calm my racing pulse.

The day had gone as well as a send off can. There were many tears, much laughter for the happy memories we could recall and warmth from the bond that we all had from loving Patty Sibley - or Anne Shelton.

The last stage of this chapter will recall the antics of arranging Anne Shelton's memorial service.

~*~

Anne being such a well known practising Catholic, I thought it would be fitting to hold her memorial service at Westminster Cathedral it being the centre of Catholicism in London, in fact England. I approached the Monsignor and it was agreed that the memorial service could be held at the Cathedral.

I had arranged a meeting with the Monsignor (I am afraid his name escapes me) and I invited Peggy Giles from the 'Not Forgotten', and Johnny Mans to accompany me, as they were to be a big part in organising this tribute.

We met with the representative from the Cathedral and started to discuss what we felt would be fitting to include in the service, also to discuss the musical tributes that were planned. Sadly, once in conversation we could see things were not going well. We were told the only songs that could be sung would be religious and we should be celebrating mainly her life as a Catholic. It was appreciated this was a very important point to take into consideration, but should we not also celebrate the part of her life as one of England's most talented daughters, and also one of the most compassionate, caring, loving, giving artists we have ever known? Putting the music topic to one side, the conversation was guided towards readings. I put forward that we had several artists in mind to do these, one being Frankie Vaughan, also stating that he would be someone who would have performed a song for her, as he had been a life long friend to Anne. The final comment from the Monsignor was unbelievable; he said that he did not think Mr Vaughan's style of music fitting, nor did it seem appropriate to have a reading from a well-noted Jewish figure at a Catholic memorial. It was at that stage that I realised this man was from another planet (no disrespect meant) and the Cathedral was not the place for us to hold Patty's memorial service. His comments seemed unjust and one of the things my aunt hated most was injustice.

It was not only the three of us who attended the meeting who were amazed and somewhat disappointed with the views of the stipulations of Westminster Cathedral, but also others who were aware of the dilemma. I would like to include at his point a letter written to the editor of 'Our Ministry' Ilford, Essex. The letter is dated 4th November 1994, and is from a gentleman called Peter Foley.

"Dear Chris,

Isn't it most extraordinary that Frankie Vaughan has been stopped from singing at the Memorial service to his friend, the distinguished singer Anne Shelton at Westminster Cathedral? His style, apparently, is deemed unsuitable.

As a result of the decision made by the Cathedral authorities, the service has been transferred by the organisers to Corpus Christi, Covent Garden.

When one considers the bland, often banal offerings both traditional and otherwise served up in our churches in the name of church music, compared to the well-loved and ever popular melodies performed for much of our lifetimes by people like Frankie Vaughan and Anne Shelton herself, one is left wondering whether our church authorities are still living in the real world.

Anne Shelton, a marvellous entertainer, a fine lady, a devoutly religious person, who, among other kindnesses, raised thousands of pounds for needy causes deserves better than this. May we hope for some sort of logical and acceptable explanation from Westminster?"

This left me with a bit of a problem. I had the date in mind, but no venue. The date was to be 10th November this seemed such an appropriate day, as it would have been her birthday.

There were numerous venues suggested none of them fitting as far as I was concerned. I really wanted it to be Catholic, but did not want to have to forgo the contributions from the artists that we had planned. With divine intervention from above it came to me Corpus Christi, Covent Garden, as this is a church which has very strong links with the Catholic Stage Guild. Perfect.

Johnny, Peggy and I met with Father John McDonald and it went very well. He was so accommodating. The service was planned, date confirmed and, luckily, I was able to hold the service on the 10th November as planned.

Here is a write up from one of the national papers:

"The Lord Lieutenant for Greater London, Field Marshall Lord Bramall, a President of the 'Not Forgotten' Association, read the lesson at the memorial service for Miss Anne Shelton held yesterday at the Church of Corpus Christi, Covent Garden.

Father John McDonald officiated, Mr John Inman read the Actors' Prayer. Tributes to Miss Shelton were paid by Maj-Gen Sir Christopher Airey of the 'Not Forgotten' Association, Mr Johnny Mans and Miss Kelly Richards (niece).

A recording of Miss Shelton singing *It Won't Be Long Till Christmas* was played. Mr Frankie Vaughan sang *All the Way*. Mr Stanley Black (piano) played *You'll Never Know* and *I'll be Seeing You*. Miss Teresa Cahill accompanied by Mr Stuart Hutchinson (piano) sang Richard Strauss's *Beim Schlafengehen* Mr Ronnie Price also took part."

There was a very large congregation and the church was full. It really was a wonderful service, and I believe my aunt would have been so touched to have been remembered so well by so many. I left the church feeling so proud of her and I just knew she was in heaven, looking down on us all with tears in her eyes....and love in her heart.

Chapter 11

'Thank You Captain Miller'

It seems such a long time ago that I embarked on my biggest venture ever, but in actual fact it was only February 2004 when I made the first step in making my dream come true. I compiled and produced a unique CD of Anne Shelton/Glenn Miller/ Bing Crosby and last but not least Jo Shelton, which I entitled *Thank You Captain Miller* A strange name you might think, but all will be revealed.

Let me take you back to the beginning of my great venture. My aunt had in her possession, since 1944 until her death in 1994, a full thirty minute 'V' disc recording that was made from a broadcast of The American Band of the Supreme Allied Command under the direction of Captain Glenn Miller. The broadcast was one of six that Anne made with Glenn. This particular one, where Anne was the guest artist singing *I'll Get By* was made on 27th July 1944. The broadcast was recorded for her as a gift by Bert Ambrose, whom I am sure at the time had no idea what a great part of history this would play.

Several times during her career she was asked if she would be willing to allow the 'V' disc broadcast to be released on record, but her response was that they were part of her personal collection and that is how, for the time being, she wanted it to stay. She told me that after her death she would like the broadcast to be made public, so that it would be a lasting memory to Glenn and herself. So this became my intention.

I remember as a child seeing these two boxes that contained what I thought to be old LPs with a funny stamp on them, and handwriting saying Glenn 1 etc….These were kept in a bureau in the billiard room at the top of the house in Dulwich. I knew from an early age that I could not touch them or play with them and only got to see them when I was with my aunts. They remained a mystery…although I was always tempted to have a look, I never did, and in fact I was still nervous to open them when they came into my possession forty-five years later. But I knew that the time had come for me to do something with the discs, albeit, as with this book it took me ten years after her death to make it all materialise, but last year I knew the time was right and I had never had that feeling before.

I wanted to have this CD, which at this stage was only in my mind, released to celebrate the 50th anniversary of D Day, also the 10th year of Anne's death. So the next thing on my agenda was, what shall I put on this new CD that I am about to compile? I did not have a clue, other than I wanted it to have the Glenn Miller/Anne Shelton broadcast, also I wanted a track of my youngest aunt Jo to be featured and I did not want *Lay Down Your Arms* to be included, as most CDs ever released of Anne's have that song, and in her later life she was not that fond of it, although it was her only number one hit. Most likely because she must have sung it 1000s of times, and it may have become somewhat of a drudge to sing. I often wonder if the Queen ever gets tired of listening to *God Save the Queen*?

My thoughts were that I wanted to produce a CD of rare recordings, as there were so many CDs that featured Anne singing her better known hits, and they all seem to have mostly the same songs. I wanted this to be a 'unique' compilation. So I spent several Sundays going through her private collection of 100s of 78 records, some of which had never been released, or at least not on albums or CDs I came up with several songs that I liked and thought people who liked her music would find pleasure in listening to. My aunt also had in her possession another 'V' disc recording, again made in 1944 of her singing a duet of *Easter Parade* with Bing Crosby, this I felt would also be popular with her fans and indeed for fans of Bing.

I came up with eighteen tracks (1 to 7 being the 30 minute

broadcast with Glenn Miller) and the others all hopefully suitable for the new CD. I asked my closest friend Di Tucker what she thought of the choice of tracks and also the idea of making the CD. She was very supportive and said that she thought the tracks were varied and showed my aunt's versatility, she said that I should go for it, and that she would back me all the way.

My dilemma was; should I go it alone or approach a small record company and hand it all over to them? I did contact a chap who specialised in the same era of music. He was very interested in taking on the project, as he had heard over the years that the broadcast of Anne and Glenn was around somewhere, but it had never surfaced. We had planned a meeting, but due to one thing and another the date was never kept, and there just did not seem to be a mutually convenient time for us to meet. At this stage I must confess I was close to giving up the idea, and just putting the tracks onto a CD for my own personal use, as the whole thing just seemed to be an awful lot of work, and I was not confident that I knew enough about the whole process to risk losing a lot of money, and making a really big mistake.

Then one morning I had a complete change of heart, thanks to a friend of mine, who I work with called Jonathan Thompson. Most mornings Jonathan and I used to spend time talking about this and that, putting the world to rights and sharing our dreams and ambitions over a cup of tea (semi skimmed milk, no sugar) and a biscuit. I told him about my abandoned dream and how much I would have loved to release this tribute to my aunt, but had given up on the idea, when he looked at me and said, "Kelly you can do this on your own, you do not need a middle man. I will help you. You are very strong willed, and you have a dream so nothing is impossible." With that I was determined to get my act together. If Jonathan and Di had so much faith in me, I must have faith in myself…….

Yellow Pages! Can you believe that good old Yellow Pages were the first port of call for my new venture? My fingers were shuffling through the pages until I hit upon 'Recording Studios', I don't know why but I was attracted to one called ASPACE.

I thought it was an omen that the first two letters were AS, and also that the studios were in Bromley, which is close to the old family home in Dulwich. Once a Londoner, always a Londoner. I really cannot tell you why I felt the need to go to London, when there were several studios close to where I lived in Brighton and Eastbourne, but I just felt it right to go back 'home' for such a venture!

I phoned ASPACE and spoke to a very helpful and patient young man called Nick. He must have thought; "I have a right one here" as I was asking all these questions, that I have no doubt made it apparent to this chap that I was a novice to the recording world. I told him what I wanted to do and he said it was possible. I asked him how much, and thought the price was acceptable, so made a date for Jonathan and I to go to Bromley. He said he did not have a 78 player to play the records on, so I would have to bring mine. Luckily as a present from Di a few years previously I was given a REGA 78 player for Christmas and without the player my attempts would have been pointless.

The time had come - 20th February 2004. Jonathan collected me from my home around 7am and we were off to Bromley. I was so nervous for our precious cargo of the 'V' Discs, other 78s and the REGA. Jonathan, bless him, had loaded his boot with such care and secured all for a safe journey. I was sort of navigator, but despite that handicap we managed to arrive at The Clan Works, Howard Road, Bromley. I was not too sure what to expect. My only visits to any recording studios had been EMI, and I knew it was unlikely to be that grand, and the anticipation was exciting.

The Clan Works was situated in a mews off a road of Victorian houses. We climbed the staircase, found the doorbell, and two seconds later we met Nick. I don't know if you have any image of what a recoding studio producer would look like, but Nick certainly met with my perceived image. Longish curly hair, unshaven by a day or so, and dressed in a rugby shirt, jeans and trainers. He then showed us into the studio....it was amazing there was so much hi-tech equipment I thought I was in EMI. Jonathan had carried up the Rega player, and the 78s leaving me to carry, and care for the Glenn Miller/ Shelton 'V' discs, which I handled with great care.

Nick set up the Rega 78 player, did his job of tuning, aligning and all the other technical computer things that he had to do. On goes the first recording that was to be the Miller broadcast. He lowered the needle with great care, to my horror the needle seemed to be jumping, the disc was not playing properly and was not at all audible. My heart sank down to my toes and back to my throat. I looked pleadingly at Jonathan with an obvious panic attack on the way. He gave me a lovely, warm, reassuring smile and said, "don't worry, it will be alright". To my relief, after several minutes (that seemed like hours) of adjustment to the arm weight and needle position it was all working well, so *Thank You Captain Miller* was on the way. Nick was not a great talker, Jonathan was sitting and taking it all in, I was left to make the tea and was talking enough for all three of us. Funny how nerves can make some people gabble on! Even stranger that no matter where you are, or how unfamiliar you are with your surroundings, it is always the woman that ends up making the tea.

We were starting to chat, as the process of converting these 78s and 'V' discs to CD seemed to be going well. I started to tell Nick the history of the broadcast and a little bit about my aunt, of whom I don't think he had ever heard, mind you, a lad his age, who had been used to working with artist from a much younger generation I would not have expected him to have been familiar with her work, but nevertheless he was very complimentary about her voice, which pleased me. Jonathan being an IT buff was very interested in the technical side of it all and engaged in several 'over my head' conversations…time for more tea.

Nick kept playing the beginning part of the broadcast over and over again. All the time he had his head phones on and was moving levers up and down, turning knobs, following indicators and constantly watching the computer monitor in front of him that had the prettiest of colours and resembled a cardiograph screen…..my heart was definitely beating at a speed, and all the time I was praying, "Please Patty let this work out."

After about forty minutes Nick said, "Do you want the broadcast to be seamless?" I had no idea what he meant, the only thing that I thought that you could get from that era that were seamless were stockings, and had to own up to my ignorance about such matters. For those of you that might not know the term 'seamless' I shall explain, for those of you that do, apologies. The whole thirty minute Glenn Miller Broadcast was copied on to seven discs, so after each disc there would obviously be a delay in the broadcast while the discs were changed, Nick by making it seamless, enabled the broadcast to be listened to as it was the first time it was aired, as a whole show....so clever!

The broadcast safely captured on the computer database, it was now time to make up the rest of the CD. Tracks chosen were-:

Don't Misunderstand Recorded 25th January 1951. Musical Director was Robert Farnon

I Fall In Love With You Everyday Recorded late 40s I do not know who was accompanying her. Song was composed by Stept.

Time May Change Recorded 22nd April 1948. Musical Director Roy Robertson.

The next three tracks are *Take Off The Coat, Siberia* (Cole Porter) and *I Ain't Got Nobody.* I am not sure who the Musical Director was on the first two, but on *I Ain't Got Nobody* she was accompanied by Johnnie Franz. I believe that these three records were recorded when she was in America for her first tour in 1950.

Now onto track 14. This was a broadcast that had to be included in this unique compilation, as it was a most collectable item. A recording of a live broadcast that Anne made with Bing Crosby on 27th August 1944. There is a lot of priceless banter between the two on this track, along with Anne and Bing singing a duet of *Easter Parade* (Berlin)

Track 15. Jo Shelton singing *If There Are Stars In My Eyes.* I believe this to have been recorded in the late 50s.

Track 16. *Village Of St Bernadette* -Recorded 1959. Musical Director Wally Stott . This is one of my most favourite songs that

Anne ever released and I just had to have it included on this CD.

Track 17. *Cross Over The Bridge* - Recorded 11th March 1954 Musical Director Ken Mackintosh.

Finally track 18. *I'll Be Seeing You.* First recording of many by Anne was 6th October 1944. On the first recording she was accompanied by the one and only Stanley Black.

So back to the day. After having been at the studio for nine hours, I was getting a little concerned as to how long we would be there for and should I have brought some supplies. I remember phoning home and saying to Di, "Hi I won't be home for a while as I am still at the recording studios." I thought that sounded so impressive. Shortly afterwards Nick appeared from this little cubicle at the back of the room and in his hand he was clutching a CD case. He held out his hand and said, "There you are one CD of *Thank You Captain Miller*"

The CD was complete. ....I had accomplished my dream. The feeling that I had was a cross between the excitement of Christmas morning, and the relief of having completed my 'A' level English Literature paper. I remember just hugging Jonathan and Nick, as I was just so excited, I was holding in my hands my completed ambition, this lasting tribute to my aunt.

On the journey home, which was about two hours, Jonathan and I were both so chatty and very elated. I held onto the CD all the way home. All I wanted to do was to get home and listen to the final version of 'my' CD. Jonathan dropped me off at home and Di and I had fish and chips and a bottle of Champagne to celebrate. I found it very hard to sleep that night, as the songs from *Thank You Captain Miller* were going through my head, and my thought was...what now?

The next morning, I woke up still on an all time high, but with a realisation that my real challenge had just begun. I now had to find somewhere to have the master copy mass produced, then I had to publicise and promote the CD, but as before in my amateurish attempts in finding a recording studio, I did not have a clue who to turn to next. The important thing was, I had the master copy!

Monday seemed to take a week to come. I must say it is very rare that one wishes the weekends over, but I could not wait to get back to my treasured 'Yellow Pages'. Not your everyday record producers main tool I am sure, but so far, good old Yellow Pages had served me well! Monday morning came and my first port of call was my monthly visit to my homeopath Sue Josling. A wonderful woman who has cured so many of my ailments, and that morning I had no idea she was going to be the saviour of the day. During our monthly chat, she was asking how my project was going. I was happy to tell her that we were at the stage to go to print, or whatever the expression should be, but that I had no idea where to go and have hundreds of CDs produced. Sue came up with the bright idea that in the Enterprise Centre (a small shopping mall in Eastbourne, East Sussex) there was a chap who advertised a similar service. Once back at my office in Eastbourne, I found out the name and number of the chap and gave him a call. What a delightful chap he was, but alas my 'little' venture as I saw it, was too mammoth a production for him. I must say that shocked me into the realisation as to what a giant project I had taken on, "Di.....Jonathan I need support"...I was shouting to myself. This gentleman turned out to be a star, although it was too big a job for him, he recommended me to a family run company also in Eastbourne called ICC Duplications. I made the initial call to a charming young man called Tim Deaves. I explained to him what was needed and like magic he came up with all the information that I needed to send me into CD production mode...look out Decca!

I made an appointment to go and see Tim and asked my mentor Jonathan to come with me. Once in Tim's office I explained to him what I wanted and he went through every option of production imaginable. I had no idea that there were so many different formats to produce a CD. Different finishes to the actual disc, different format for the CD sleeve and, of course, different types of art work. All mind blowing to a novice! Although I had no idea what I was doing, I knew what I wanted the finished article to look like. I wanted a background of Union Jack and Stars and Stripes, with a picture that I had of Anne when she was singing with Glenn in 1944, and of course a picture of Glenn. I also went armed with all the pictures that I wanted to be included in the insert to give Tim an idea of how many pages would be needed. We met with a lad called Sam who was going to do the art work etc…I was amazed and felt very old when he told me he had neither heard of Anne Shelton or Glenn Miller, still I must admit I had never heard of anyone he mentioned that he had recently done art work for. I produced my pictures for the insert. One of which was of Glenn Miller that I had photographed from a book, all the others of my aunts and Bing Crosby were from my own personal collection. Lesson number two, Sam informed me that I could not just use 'any old picture' that I did not have copyright of, so the one of Glenn was not suitable…..then Tim went on to say that they could not publish the CD without a licence from MCPS. "Who on earth are MCPS?" I asked. I was informed that those initials stood for Mechanical – Copyright Protection Society Ltd, and I would need to pay royalties to them before I could be granted a licence to have the CD produced. So, after about an hour discussing all these hurdles and obstacles, I was again thinking… "this is going to be such hassle, do I have the energy to go ahead with this?" Tim was very helpful and gave me all the information that I needed to contact MCPS, which is something I would need to do before my venture could go any further. Jonathan and I left and I was feeling exhausted at the prospect of filling in the very long form that I had been given regarding all the information that was needed re writers/publishers/and owners of all the tracks that were featured on the CD. Plus the fact I would need to contact the BBC to pay a copyright fee to use a picture of Mr Miller. I said to Jonathan, "I don't think I want to go ahead with this." He told me not to be so silly and that I could not give up after the first obstacle, he also said that everyone would have to go through the same process, and look how many CDs there are around!

I survived the ordeal. I phoned the BBC archives department and they were also very helpful. I paid the copyright fee and was allowed to use a very similar picture of Glenn Miller to the one I had photographed from the book, but this time I could legally use it. I then filled in the form with as much information that I had about the other tracks on the CD and sent that off to MCPS. I paid the royalties up front to MCPS, and was awarded my licence to manufacture the CD. I must say I thought it a bit harsh that I had to pay the royalties before I had even had the CD produced, not to mention sold a copy, still at least it was now all legal and I would be able to go into production.

We went back to ICC, decided what CD finish we wanted, what sleeve inlay was required, and the layout of the insert. All systems go. The master CD was then on its way to Sony in Austria to be mass produced. It needed a catalogue number, which it was given ASCD1…seemed appropriate.

The next decision to be made was a date for release. I told Tim that the date that I had in mind was 23rd April 2004. There were two reasons for choosing this particular date. Firstly it was my birthday and secondly St George's Day, a good day to release a CD of one of England's best singers I thought. Tim said he thought it was achievable, so the 23rd April was the date we were going for. As I have said this was a tribute to Anne and Glenn, so it was very important to me that this CD be released in time to commemorate D Day in the June.

Those following weeks seemed to take an age to go. I realised that producing the CD was the easy bit, now I had to promote and sell it. I did not want to approach the larger stores and record companies, I wanted to keep it small and personal and for it only to be available through me.

One thing that I had decided is that I wanted to give some of the money from any sales to charities that were close to my aunt's heart. I thought it would be fitting for these charities to be linked with the forces, so I approached The 'Not Forgotten' Association and the RAF through RAFATRAD. Both these organisations agreed to promote the CD through their magazines which are circulated to their members and I agreed to donate 10% of the sales to both charities. I also approached the British Legion with the same offer, but alas they were not interested. So much planned, but not a CD in sight. I phoned Tim about the second week in April and he assured me all was going well….Please God..let it stay that way!

My next step was to try and get the local papers interested in my story. I needed to let people know this unique CD was available. I am not by nature a pushy person, so selling myself to the press did not come easy to me, I found it very embarrassing, but knew it had to be done, I needed the publicity, as *Thank You Captain Miller* was not going to sell itself. This reminds me, I have not told you how I came to name the CD. Some of you who already have a copy may have noticed that during the broadcast Glenn introduces Anne by saying….. "Well here is a little lady, lovely to look at, delightful to hear Miss Anne Shelton" and then my aunt responds by saying "Thank You Captain Miller" So there you are, the CD was named. Rather fitting I thought.

I had a phone call from Tim informing me that the CD would be delivered to me on 21st April. The whole thing was actually coming together.

Fate was most surely on my side, as one day at work I happened to bump into a chap I had known since my aunt's demise, in fact he bought her house in Stunts Green from me, after her death in 1994. His name is Roger Thomas and at that time he was the chairman for East Sussex County Council, for whom I also worked. We got chatting and I mentioned the CD to him, and how I needed to advertise, advertise, advertise…Roger used to work for the BBC, and also had a history of journalism in Hong Kong. A lovely chap, who came up with several helpful suggestions, names to call and also offered to write an article about the time he interviewed Anne in Hong Kong. True to his word, he came up trumps and I got me a write up in the local papers, which included the Eastbourne Gazette, Argus and Eastbourne Herald. We were on the move.

On the 21st April 2004 for obvious reasons I had taken leave. I was at home showered and dressed by 7.00 awaiting my delivery. The day had come and *Thank You Captain Miller* was coming home. Unfortunately Di was unable to take the day off due to work commitments, so that left me and Willow (our very adorable, too intelligent Border collie) to wait for the delivery lorry? van? I really had no idea what a large quantity of CDs would look like. Or by what means they would be delivered.

The rather large lorry arrived. Pleasant enough driver asked me where I wanted the pallet put. I was fearful just how big this pallet would be, but thankfully it was a manageable size and I asked the driver to leave it up the drive. I then spent some time carrying the twenty large boxes of CDs into our dining room, which was soon to become the CD sorting office.

I was so eager to see what the final product would look like, I opened one of the boxes and there was 'my' CD. It was done and ready to be sold.

Later that day, I had a phone call at home from a charming lady who I did not know, asking me if I was Anne Shelton's niece. How strange I thought, as she went on to say how she would like to buy a copy of the new CD *Thank You Captain Miller*. I took her address, it looked like I had my first sale. I wondered how this lovely lady had my home number as we are ex-directory? Then over the next couple of hours I had thirty calls....I was amazed but so pleased, my project had taken off......then Di came home with a copy of the local paper that had been released that day, and bless them they had put my home number in the article, which solved the mystery! I was so excited about seeing my name and picture in the paper that I went out and bought several copies, my claim to fame.

I am happy to say that over the last year the sales of the CD have been very good and they are still only available through me via the Anne Shelton website or by post. I have resisted the temptation to release them into the retail chain.

Over the year most of the sales have come via the Royal Mail and almost every order has been accompanied with a letter or a card with some comment regarding Anne. People have been so kind, and it is obvious from the correspondence, that she is still highly thought of, not just as a very talented singer/performer, but also praised for being the lovely lady that she was. She made a lot of people very happy and they still hold happy memories of her. I am not ashamed to say that some of these kind words brought tears to my eyes.

It was my intention to send a compliment slip out with every order, with a short message of thanks. I am happy to say that I have been able to do this and have formed some interesting contacts with some of her fans. Several of these are mentioned later on in this book.

I will conclude this chapter by saying that our dining room is still the Anne Shelton Fan Club post room.....

Information regarding *Thank You Captain Miller.*
CD is available by sending a cheque for £12.04 (£10.99 + £1.05pp) made payable to Kelly Richards, to, PO BOX 160. Hailsham, East Sussex BN27 4YF

Also available is a CD that I have more recently released entitled *My Pal Jo.* This unique disc features both Anne and Jo singing on the same track, *Tread Softly* and also features Jo as well as Anne, singing other songs.

My Pal Jo is also available for the same price (£12.04) and by sending a cheque to the same address as above.

Chapter Twelve

The People's Tribute....
the fans have their say.

I decided that the greatest tributes that can be paid to Anne are those that have come from her life long fans and other stars who knew and worked with her. This final chapter is just that. I have been so overwhelmed over the last twelve years with the tributes, letters and e-mails regarding her popularity. It is so uplifting to know how fondly she is remembered.

I have compiled extracts from genuine letters giving accounts of memories and meetings with Anne by her much loved fans. All of these letters are as precious to me as they would have been to my aunt. Many of you reading this will find your name and memories, so I would like to take this opportunity to say the biggest thank you for all of your kind comments, which have been an inspiration to me in writing this biography. So let's take a trip down Memory Lane.

The first account has been written by Jim Woolley.

Jim, has also contributed much to this book with his knowledge of Anne's early career, in fact the whole of her career.

"I guess I was just about twelve or thirteen when I first heard Anne Shelton singing with the Ambrose Orchestra on the wireless. I never quite knew why it was called a wireless because when one looked into the back of the receiver there seemed to be hundreds of wires. My dad wasn't ever musically inclined, unlike me, but he did enjoy listening to the Ambrose Orchestra, which he had done since the early 30s. I of course am writing about the very early 40s in fact 1940, so it naturally follows that when I was around I also listened. If I remember correctly the weekly broadcasts used to be on a Friday, which was always referred to as bath night, reasons for which I will not go into! Anyway the occasion that I am referring to may not have been Anne's first broadcast, but it was not long after it. The vocalists we had been hearing with Ambrose were people like Sam Browne, Jack Cooper, Elsie Carlisle and sometimes Evelyn Dall, but during this broadcast Anne was announced as "my new young vocalist, Anne Shelton". She sang *Flamingo* and *Begin the Beguine*. I thought "wow! what a voice", and my dad surprisingly agreed with me, because in those days parents did not always like what their children did, although I do not think there was such an age gap musically speaking as there is these days. From then on I always made sure that I looked out for when Anne was going to be broadcasting and when I saved enough pocket money bought my first record (a 78 Shellac) of her singing *Humpty Dumpty Heart*. Unfortunately only one side was by Anne, the other side was a song called *Moonlight Cocktails* by Alan Kane

I was hooked on Anne's wonderful voice from the very beginning and remained so right up to her untimely death in July 1994. The reason I think for this is because she was so versatile. I usually found that a lot of singers then were only suited to one style of song, whereas Anne could deal with the slow sentimental, upbeat jazz and also comedy numbers. This was amazing for someone of such a young age, it was hitherto unheard of. I remember the first time that I met Anne. It was in 1951 after her triumphant tour of the U.S.A. She was appearing in variety at the Finsbury Park Empire. Also on the bill was a very young man named Max Bygraves who was billed as Britain's newest comedy star. When the show ended I decided to stand outside the stage door hoping to get a glimpse of Anne as she was leaving. It turned out to be better than a glimpse, for soon after I arrived at the stage door, a gentleman came out to ask me who I was hoping to see, the chap in question happened to be David Reid who was her fiancé and manager. He told me to follow him and took me straight to Anne's dressing room and introduced me to her, and Mrs

Shelton, her mother. I stayed for about fifteen minutes, we talked about her American tour, and that evening's show. As I got up to go we shook hands and she kissed me on the cheek. I will never forget that evening. I still have the programme bearing her autograph, although it is a bit battered now. The programme cost me three old pence and my seat in the grand circle cost me three shillings and sixpence. I met Anne and several members of her family over the years, she was always very kind, without any airs and graces, and had the ability to put you at ease immediately.

Two songs I particularly liked to hear her sing on stage were *That Old Feeling* and *Birth of the Blues*, there were many others of course.

I think we are very fortunate that we can avail ourselves of the many records she made during her career, and for this reason she will never die. Long may the memories stay with us."

~*~

The next dear lady, who has so kindly agreed to give her memories of Anne, is Phyllis Kitchen, a fan for many years, who became a dear friend to Anne and the family.

"The first time I heard Anne sing was on a programme on the wireless called 'Ambrose and Anne' and from then on she was top of my list. I never missed a programme, or show of hers if I could help it. After 'Ambrose and Anne' there came lots of programmes and series all starring Anne Shelton, and I saw all of them. 'Anne to You', 'Hit Parade' (with Bruce Trent), 'Double Top' (with Alfred Marks) to name but a few. I was so thrilled when I heard she was coming in person to the Alhambra Theatre here in Bradford. I can still remember the first song she sang on stage, it was *The Trolley Song,* she also sang; *Begin The Beguine, It Had To Be You, For You, Give Me Five Minutes More* and *My Happiness.* After the show we went round to the stage door for her autograph and she said that the next time that we went to see her to come back stage again, before the show. You can imagine how I felt then!

After that first meeting, my mum and I went to see her at every theatre we could physically get to, they included theatres in Leeds, Manchester, Blackpool and Morecambe.

I remember one time when we went to Morecambe to see a show Anne was in, during the morning, just before lunch we went to the theatre to find out where the stage door was, so that we would know where to go after the show to get to it. To get to the back of the theatre we had to go down this snicket. Well as would be our luck, me and mum got half way down the snicket and this car was coming the other way, so we had to stand to one side to let it pass, but, the car did not move, the horn sounded. We were just wondering what we should do, when the door opened and out came Anne. She asked where we were going, we told her and she told us where the stage door was. She then asked us what our plans were? I explained how we were going to get some lunch, then she said, "well get into the car and come back and have lunch with me at the hotel. I could not believe it.

As time went on we went to see Anne wherever we could. Years went by and we stayed in contact by phone and letter mostly. The last time I saw Anne was at Leeds Town Hall where she topped the bill in a forties night concert. Anne was great as usual. My mum always said, "a show without her was a show without a star", and I agree.

The last time I spoke to Anne was on the Tuesday before she passed away, she was getting ready for her summer concert at Buckingham Palace on the Wednesday, which she organised for the 'Not Forgotten' Association. I didn't know then, that in a few days time we were to loose her. That day 31st July was a sad day for all of us and it is a day I shall never forget. I have a mass said for her every year on the anniversary of her death, and her birthday and I always will while I am alive.

She was at ease singing any type of song, but then it was the singer that made the song, not the song that made the singer. I often wonder how many of today's pop stars will be around in 54 years time, as long as Anne's career spanned? For me there has only been one queen of song – Anne Shelton."

~*~

May Smethurst, a friend and fan for many years........ Here are her memories.

"I left school in Greater Manchester in 1945 at the age of fourteen and was already into pop songs, Anne being my favourite singer. I immediately became a serious fan, but could not have believed then that my support would be lifelong, as was our friendship.

I would often write to Anne for autographs and photos, which she never failed to forward, and I went to see her shows whenever she appeared in Manchester. As I grew older I was allowed to travel further afield and remained a staunch follower.

In the late forties there was a weekly radio programme called 'Hit Parade' with Anne, Bruce Trent and The George Mitchell Choir all as regular singers. Songs such as *Riders In The Sky, Lavender Blue, A- Your Adorable* and Anne's own *Wedding of Lilli Marlene* were very popular at the time. I would never go out the evenings that the show was on until it had finished, as I used to write down all the song titles in my 'little black book' as Anne called it. In fact I have three such books in which I wrote down the song titles each time I heard her on the radio or television. Anne and her songs were my life.

Another programme I enjoyed was called 'Anne's Song Parade' on Radio Luxemburg. It ran for three series between 1957 -1960. Her signature tune was *With a Smile and a Song.* That tune often introduced Anne on stage as well, and was played at her entrance and exit from stage.

When I heard that a Fan Club was to be formed, I was the first to join and that is why I call myself 'Anne's Number One Fan'. Sometime later Anne asked three of us members if we would like to take over the running of the club, as she felt that we could do a better job (Anne was very busy, and did not have as much time to devote to the Fan Club as she would have liked). Without hesitation we took it on as a labour of love in our spare time.

In December 1961, we three fan club organisers arranged a party at London's Café Royal to celebrate Anne's 'Twenty One

Years in Show Business'. We had no idea what to buy for her, so we asked her what she would like, and her response was that if we were going to be kind enough to buy her something, she really would love a medal of St Bernadette to add to the many religious medals that were on a gold bracelet which she had had since the start of her career. Fans from all over the country attended and I was the lucky one to present the medallion. Needless to say we all had a lovely time with our 'Star'.

I thought the following might be of interest that Anne Shelton and Cyril Fletcher were the two celebrities who took part in the final broadcast of 'Workers Playtime' which came from Cook's Corrugated Case Factory in Hatfield, Herts, on 6th October 1964. You might think this is useless information, but I thought it was great at the time because Anne often sang on the programme, and she deserved to be chosen for the last broadcast. Incidentally the three songs that she sang were *How Soon,* ' *Cried For You* and *If Ever I Would Leave You.* These are some of the memories I will always cherish."

~*~

I was delighted back in 2004 to have contact with two very lovely people, Arthur and Joan Featherstone from Suffolk. Listen to their story in their own words.

11th September 2004.

"We are always interested when the name of Anne Shelton comes up. In late 1941 together with the lady who has been my wife for the last 58 years, we saw a matinee performance at the Phoenix Theatre in Charing Cross Road, London of a show called 'The Ambrose Merry-Go-Round', this had Anne with the future legend George Shearing, plus Teddy Foster and Carl Barittau. Anne sang a song that we had not heard before, but which became a part of our life forever. The song was *Yours* and always after that we both signed all of our letters with *Yours* surrounded by kisses underneath our signatures, and it still features now on our cards to each other. Anne Shelton has been part of our life and love ever since. I was in the RAF at the time and went to India at the beginning of 1942 returning for Christmas 1945. We married in 1946 and the last time we saw Anne in person was at the Ipswich Hippodrome in 1947. Upon contacting her there, she was kind enough to send us an autographed photo "To Baby Paula" as our daughter was only a few months old at the time.

We followed her career with great interest and it was with great sadness we heard of her death. I have a letter she wrote to me after we had seen her at the Phoenix Theatre and the programme of the show.

Thank you for reading this, I am now in my 84th year and my wife Joan is in her 80th. Good luck with the CD. I shall be asking my grandson to look up the Anne Shelton website for me, as it sounds interesting."

~*~

I corresponded with Arthur, and one of my questions was did Arthur and Joan have a copy of 'Yours'? If not, my quest would be to obtain one for them. Their reply was as follows.

September 17th 2004

"Thank you for your letter, I must say that your query of did we have a recording of *Yours* came as a big surprise. The only copy we have is the old 78 that I must have bought before I went to India in 1942, I have searched and searched but no luck in finding a copy. I must say the 78 which we have is of no use, other than a memento of our visit to the Phoenix. So please may we take advantage of your kind offer to search through your collection for us, it would be treasured should you be able to supply us with a copy."

It was not an easy task, but I managed to track down a copy of 'Yours' and had it copied onto a CD for Arthur and Joan. It gave me so much pleasure to be able to do this. I was so excited I had to phone to let them know that I had the song, which was soon to be theirs, to keep forever.

28th October 2004

"My, what a surprise you gave me the other evening when you phoned! I nearly dropped the phone when you said who you were! Thank you so much for calling and again for obtaining a copy of *Yours* for us. We received it yesterday and it has been played several times since. Memories flooded back to both of us, of a very young Anne singing her heart out just for us (or so it seemed) on a cold October afternoon in 1941. It will always be our song......Thank you again for all the trouble you took, you must be, I am sure, a very caring lady."

I am happy to say that I am still in contact with Arthur and Joan.

~*~

Lee Stevens is a presenter on BBC Southern Counties Radio, here is the letter I received from him in June 04.

"Dear Kelly.

Please get the CD to me as soon as possible as I will play it on BBC Southern Counties where I do a weekly hour long show. Anne being a personal friend of mine gets regular plays. I miss her like hell, she was probably the best singer we have ever had, I say this looking at a faded picture taken with her, which is on my wall. Good luck with the CD and listen into Southern Counties, Tuesday's 2-3 The Bill Buckley Show to hear me."

This is the second letter from Lee. June 04

"Thank you for the copy of *Thank You Captain Miller.* It is very good and Jo should have pursued a career in singing, I never realised just how good she was.

This CD is really a collector's item, I am really impressed. As far as I am concerned she was always the best singer of that period and will never be forgotten whilst I play her records on radio.

Listen in......Sincerely Lee

I do hope I am not boring you. Please be truthful, if I am, stop reading now and have a moan. Believe me there have been so many letters, that I have included just a few.....but here I go again.

"I was so delighted to read the story of your aunt Anne Shelton. As I opened the pages and saw Anne's face and I started to read, my scalp started to tingle. The reason for this is that she had such a wonderful voice and the article brought back memories of when I was young, about six or seven, when I stayed with my aunt and uncle. My uncle was in the Navy during the war, and just after the war I remember my aunt cooking breakfast listening to the radio, your Aunt Anne was singing *Sailor* and my aunt was singing along to it. These are good memories for me. What a trooper your aunt was, you must be so proud to be her niece, keep up the good work."

Ian Wainham, Lancs

"I heard on Southern Counties Radio last night about the new CD of your aunts. It is so good that you are working hard to keep Anne's name alive, indeed one of the greatest singers this country has ever had, thank you for keeping Anne's name in the public eye."

Denis Lownds, Sussex

"Thank you for allowing us the privilege in sharing your aunt's music with you. I remember her from the 1950s, as on leaving school I worked in a gramophone record shop and we sold lots of Anne's records, some will ask; "what's a gramophone record?"

Peter Rees, East Sussex

The next correspondence came by e-mail from a lady who lives in Australia now, but was born in good old Blighty! Her name is Maria Aly. Her request follows.....

December 12th 2004

"Hello there... I have been searching for years, (literally) for a copy of Anne's *Dancing With Tears In My Eyes*' that she released in the 60s and it was in the 'hit parade'...

I was born and raised in UK, (Hertfordshire) and my mother adored Anne Shelton.. "she has a voice like a bell", she would say and I bought the single as they were known then, on Decca label I think? We would play it over and over. I remember seeing her on the TV singing that song, which was reasonably up-tempo, but beautiful nevertheless. I have 'surfed' about every Anne Shelton website I come across and it would appear that the only CD available with this particular song is *Now Hear This* from the See for Miles label. Sadly, no one is selling it! Please, please would you be able to help me. My mother died the year after I emigrated to Australia and to hear that song playing full blast in my lounge, with my children and grand-children around me, would mean more to me than I can explain. Can you help me?

Kind Regards
Maria Aly

I was very happy to be able to do this for Maria; in fact, I also had 'tears in my eyes' when I read her correspondence.

Hi Kelly,

I know no words that would *accurately* describe my feelings of appreciation for your kindness.

I have just listened to *Dancing With Tears In My Eyes* and that's exactly what I had...Tears in my eyes....sobbing uncontrollably whilst laughing almost hysterically.... I 'saw' my home in England and 'heard' my mother humming along and asking me to, 'play it again!'...So I did....cannot remember how many times, but the neighbours know the words now I'm sure. What can I say? Thank you sounds so inadequate...I wish I could explain how your thoughtful, caring deed has enriched my life...To read my name on the same CD as 'Anne Shelton' is humbling to say the least and brings me incredible joy! I will cherish your gift for as long as I live and may God bless you for being you! (playing it again!!). There has not been, and will never be, a voice quite like Anne Shelton…. What a tone! I shall of course listen to the entire CD as soon as I've heard that track a bit more!

Music has played an enormous part in my existence without which I may have not endured several episodes in life! My CD collection covers just about every mood. I learned piano from the age of five and taught myself guitar and clarinet in later years. Do you play an instrument, or perhaps sing? I love to sing, but have lost voice quality due to years of smoking (and screaming at the children no doubt!).

If you have time, I would love to correspond with you and look forward to reading Anne's biography…My sympathy lies with folk who have amazingly 'never heard of her'… Did she have any children?

You know Kelly, there are not many people left in the world like you, selfless, courteous and beneficent. It's times like this that I miss living in England…(emigrated in Jan 1970, 18 years old, married and six months pregnant!) But my family is here so although alone (apart from Louie) *freedom* is conditional I guess.

I have three daughters: Samantha, 34, who has four children, two boys aged 15 and 14 and two girls, 11 and 8. Tennille, 28, two girls (4 next month) and 2 and a boy due in two weeks!

And Heidi, 26, divorced, no children. They all live in South Australia at the moment but Sam and family are relocating to Queensland (which may as well be overseas…) On the 7th Jan and I'm dreading it….I miss them already you know?

I return to work on Tues 4th after a two week Chrissie break, thankfully. And surprisingly, I enjoy my job. I re-entered the workforce after more than twenty-six years in July 2003. It was challenging to say the least!

It has occurred to me that you, as a writer must think my literary skills lacking somewhat!

I apologise if this e mail is a 'tad' tedious, but feel the impulse to tell you a little about me, with the hope that you may reciprocate.

Thank you again Kelly…Yours truly, Maria

~*~

Another interesting letter that I received was from a very talented young lady called Clare Cunliffe. Clare wrote to me in April 04, requesting a copy of the CD Thank You Captain Miller asking for a speedy delivery if possible, as she was appearing as Anne Shelton.......Clare tells her story.

26th April 2004

"Please could you forward me a copy of *Thank You Captain Miller* as soon as possible as I am playing Anne Shelton in a new show starting May 18th and feel that the 'V' disc recording of Anne and Glenn will help me considerably with her character......"

The very next day the CD was despatched to Clare with a letter to wish her well with her part. Her reply....

2nd May 2004

"Thank you for your quick delivery of the CD. I played it straight away and it is wonderful. It is so good to have a clear recording of her speaking voice as well as her singing, as this will help me with my lines, as well as the songs. The show is called 'American Patrol' and is all about Glenn Miller, his life and his band. I am appearing as Anne Shelton in a cameo role. The scene is set at the 'Queensbury All Service Club', The play is set between June 44 and December 44.

The play runs from 20th May until 22nd May, at the Mayflower Theatre Southampton. The musical director is Don Hunt who worked with Anne in her later years.

I would be thankful if you could send me any pointers you can offer me on Anne. How she moved, any idiosyncrasies she made have had....or anything that might help me.

Let me know if you would like to come to the show, and maybe we could meet up, I am sure Don would love to meet you.

Many thanks for your help, I hope I can do your auntie Anne justice....."

I went to see the show 'American Patrol' which was excellent. Clare played the part of Anne very well, my aunt would have been most impressed. Clare has a lovely voice and I am sure we will be hearing more of her...a name to look out for!

~*~

The following are a few extracts from letters received:

"I pride myself in having known Anne very well from talking to her in Selfridges, also attending concerts in various places, then getting to know David and Jo by my being back stage after many concerts.

We always received Christmas cards from Anne, Jo and David, and I have them all safely kept in an album. We attended Anne's concerts at Margate, Alert Hall, Croydon, Windsor, and Yeovil to mention only a few and often Anne would dedicate a song to us when she knew we were in the audience.

To have known Anne was to love her and I shall always cherish fond memories of her kindness and open friendship with us.

I did meet Eileen on one occasion, and may also have met you? Our last meeting with Anne was Weston-Super-Mare early in 94. We have wonderful memories of a lovely lady. I look forward to receiving the CD which I am sure will give us a great deal of pleasure"

Philip Reeves, Somerset

Just a few more?
"Your aunt is one of my most favourite singers and, I think, one of the greatest vocalists the UK has ever heard or produced."

Mr Endacott, London

"Many, many thanks for sharing your aunt's music with us her fans. I only hope you will find it in your heart to release some more."

Jean Villa

"My friend has ordered me a copy of your CD *Thank You Capt Miller*, as I have been a fan of Anne's since the 40s. I have also had the privilege of meeting her at one of The 'Not Forgotten' Association shows at Buckingham Palace. I took an American singer there as a guest, his name was Joe Francis. On the bill with Anne was Ruby Murray and Alan Randel, we all sat down with Royalty and had a wonderful meal....We shall all miss her as she was such a lovely lady, but her voice goes on every day of the year, through 78 records, LPs and CDs

Phil Clarke, Havant

"Please send me the CD of our lovely Anne. She was the sweetheart of the forces, ask any Second World War veteran, of which I am one."

Ken Fordyce, Northants

"I was so pleased with the CD that I would like to order another one for my special friends, one of which met Anne at a Buckingham Palace show and went on stage with her. I have told him to write to you and tell you all about it, as I thought you might be interested in the story.

I have always admired Anne's wonderful, wonderful voice. She had such sincere feeling when she sang any song"

Ron Muirhead, Edinburgh.

"What a lovely voice Anne had, that beautiful contralto. I have a number of her CDs and have happy memories of hearing her before, during and after the 1939-45 war. A truly great lady."

John Long, Kent

"What a wonderful thoughtful thing to do Kelly, a fine tribute to your aunt Anne Shelton O.B.E, who was a remarkable person. Thanks also for the acknowledgment to the 'Not Forgotten'

(George Simmons, Ex Gunner RA Birmingham)

~*~

The following correspondence I would like to share with you all. It is very important to me, as it is an e-mail from a young man called Simon Robinson who spurred me on to compile the CD *My Pal Jo*. I had wanted to have both Anne and Jo featured on one CD for years, but never got around to it until I received the e-mail from Simon. See what you think!

4ᵗʰ February 2004

Hello,

I received the wonderful CD today! I am 22 and while I still enjoy today's music, I adore the 1940s music and especially Anne Shelton. I love Anne Shelton's singing whether it be a 40s record with Ambrose or a 50s/60s record. Her voice was amazing I love her style and that powerful voice, the lovely ballads or real jazz/swing songs! A real star! I have a DVD of her in a film 'Miss London Ltd'.

I had never before heard her sister Jo Shelton who also has a remarkable voice, *If There Are Stars In My Eyes* is a lovely song and her singing is lovely. Did she cut any more records other than that one? I'd love to know? Is Jo Shelton still alive?

This CD is wonderful, from the atmospheric Glenn Miller broadcast to the cool *Take Off The Coat* to the lovely *Village of St.Bernadette* and it was great to hear Jo Shelton, incidentally when was it recorded, I thought circa 1950?

Thank you for a prompt service and a very special item! I will play this to my friends and I know my Grandparents will love it when I take it round for them to hear. My great uncle Bill played her 78s in North Africa during the war and tells how the sand used to scratch them, and my Gran used to listen to her programme in London. Of all the versions of *A Nightingale Sang in Berkeley Square*, there has never been a version as lovely as Anne Shelton's."

You can see I am sure how inspiring that correspondence was to me. I replied immediately, and I am happy to say, so did Simon!

"Hello Kelly,

I can understand how proud you must be of them both! I am so pleased you are working on another CD. It will be excellent and how marvelous that you are working on Anne Shelton's biography! I have always thought it was a shame that she didn't have a biography and know it will make a very interesting read! Have you seen any of Anne Shelton's films, I am just about to buy 'Bees in Paradise' which I believe Jo Shelton was in. There's a lovely piece of interview and an all-to-brief glimpse of her in concert on a documentary video 'The Women Who Went To War', which I am sure you have seen. Do you know of any other interviews of her available on VHS/DVD? About eight years ago or so, I heard a radio programme with my Nan (she is 81 now) which may have been a radio documentary on Anne Shelton and she is introduced in that very BBC 1940s style manner with a number called *Let The Curtain Come Down* and I have never seen it on a compilation, have you ever heard it?

Lastly I must say what a lovely tribute it is to both of your aunts that you do keep their memory alive and provide such unheard gems for fans like myself and very best wishes for the book and new CD- I can't wait!

Best wishes Simon."

~*~

Well, I must say that after receiving that second e-mail from Stephen, it was like a bolt from heaven that struck me! "Move it, move it." I thought to myself. I spent the next week compiling the CD, approached my producers ICC Productions in Eastbourne, gave them the compilation in various formats, from CD to cassette, and by the wonders of modern technology, and with the expertise of ICC's technician Mark, the first was ready within a week. I loved it! A couple of changes were needed, but in all it was fantastic. You might have picked up that I am a very emotional person, and I must say that when I heard both of my much loved aunts Patty (Anne

*in case you have forgotten) and Josie (family
name for Jo) sing Tread Softly, I was so emotional that I thought
to myself, even if I don't sell one copy, the cost to produce this
CD is worth it to me, just for my own satisfaction in hearing
them sing together. My Pal Jo was released on 23rd April 2006.*

*The last recollection comes from a very dear friend of ours,
Jayne Jolliffe. As you will see in the book, Jayne was the first
person to arrive at Anne's home the day she died.*

"Having become a close friend of Kelly and Di, I knew it was
only a matter of time before I would meet Anne Shelton. I was
completely ignorant of her career and style of music so decided I
had better find out a bit about her. I duly asked my parents if they
had heard of her "heard of her?" Said my father, "she was
fantastic". I had unknowingly opened the floodgates and proceeded
to hear about this beautiful woman with the most amazing voice
who had played such an important role in keeping up the spirits of
the nation during the years of the Second World War. I only had to
look at the dreamy, faraway look in my father's eye and to listen
to my mother rave about her wonderful voice to begin to understand
what a star Anne had been at the height of her career. On my next
visit to Kelly and Di's home, I asked whether they had any of
Anne's records that I could listen to. Kelly played me a track from
a CD of Anne singing a song entitled *Cross Over The Bridge*.
The hairs on the back of my neck immediately stood up as the
room was filled with the most beautiful, rich voice I had ever heard.
I was immediately a fan.

I was fortunate to meet Anne on many occasions and always
looked forward to seeing her. She was large, beautiful and
glamorous, the sort of person you would want to scoop you up and
cradle you in her large bosom if feeling unhappy. She was warm
and welcoming and had a way of making her guests feel important
and special. During one of the first times that I met her, she spoke
to me about my very dear friend Chris who had died of cancer,
whom Anne had never met. She told me that Chris and she had
shared something in common, a love of wristwatches. It transpired

that Anne, like Chris had quite a collection. I later mentioned this to Kelly, she had no idea how Anne knew about my friend's love of watches, as she had never mentioned it to her. Whether she had a 'gift' relating to psychic matters, I do not know, but I do know what she said and how uncanny it was.

Another occasion that I met Anne was at her home in Sussex, when I popped in to see that all was alright with her and Eileen whilst Kelly and Di were on holiday. She immediately disappeared upstairs and returned with a large roll of bank notes. She made reference to Chris and asked me to give the money to the Cancer Relief Macmillan Fund. There were hundreds of pounds in my hand and I was more than a little surprised given that no conversation had taken place before this extremely generous gesture. She was adamant however that I should do as she asked; she simply wanted to make a donation.

The last time I saw her she had invited me to accompany her, Kelly and Di for her next performance which was to be for the 'Not Forgotten' Association at Buckingham Palace, but this was not to be. It was a great privilege to have been invited and an even greater one to have known her".

To finish off, this rather long chapter, I thought it would be interesting to contact some of the stars who worked with Anne on her last show at Buckingham Palace, and ask them for their memories of her. This I managed to do. The first artiste that I spoke with was Ray Alan (without Lord Charles on this occasion) he said the following.

"She was still bouncy at the show on the 27th July, which was just three days before she died. Having worked with her many times over the years, she was always such fun and had such a memory for naughty poems and songs, she was always laughing. When you went into her dressing room it was like a shrine, as she had a little altar there, with statues.....lovely lady."

I then phoned the number that was in Anne's address book

for the Beverley Sisters. I was amazed that the phone was answered by one of the Bevs, as Anne's address book was very old and I thought out of date. I did not think to ask which of the sisters I was speaking to, but I think it was Joy, as she mentioned that the twins were with her. Here is her account.

"We loved her. She had unusual talent and an unusual voice for a youngster, she was unique. She was very close to her sister and always called her darling. I remember one time that we were both appearing at a Royal Command Performance. We were backstage together and I was so nervous and I told Anne this, she said "Don't be ridiculous, you are a star, go on and be one". That was so kind of her and it gave me so much confidence. I will always remember that.

Anne was always in Vera Lynn's shadow sadly, I think it was because Vera was lucky in as much as she was established right at the start of the war and Anne came along later.

At the 'Not Forgotten' shows at Buckingham Palace, I remember how lovely she always was, very sympathetic to our needs and very competent in her organizing of the shows. At the last show on the 27th, she told me that she was ready to go; she had had enough of life. She was a warm loving person to everyone and she had a rich fulfilling life."

The very talented and charming Rosemary Squires MBE had this to say.

"Our paths never crossed until the early eighties when, during a summer season when I was co-starring with Tommy Trinder, (well someone had to do it) he and I shared a judging panel for 'Miss Skegness' and Anne was booked for the cabaret. They knew each other well and the spontaneous banter once she recognized him in the audience showed that Tommy had met his match! As an admirer I was thrilled to meet her later and I like to think that was the night that the mutual admiration society was born.

Our next meeting was far less glamorous in a Service Station on the M1 snowbound on our way to separate gigs in the North. I never did find out whether she made it to her show.

Later Anne phoned inviting me to appear in one of her 'Not Forgotten' Association Concerts at Buckingham Palace. She assured me that it would not be an improvised auditorium in the stables as was my last concert there. Anne had shared that experience and once she was in charge things had to change. This time we had a posh marquee, good staging, lighting and sound. Characteristically, Anne had things organized and earned the admiration of all the artistes. The only blip was that it had rained heavily before the marquee was erected and I can see us now shuffling around with plastic bags over our high heeled shoes.

We always kept in touch on the phone as with her sister Jo through the 'highs' and the 'lows' and maybe that helped. I hope so. Like all ladies of mature years we would put the world to rights!

Anne's unique talent, her stature and dignity were tempered by great warmth of personality. Along with her many fans we miss her greatly and yet she lives – her recordings are still in catalogues. That says it all for me."

I would like to thank Ivor Spencer MBE for the letter that he sent me relating to his memories of Anne. Ivor worked with Anne at the 'Not Forgotten' shows at Buckingham Palace. The following explains his role.

I am a professional Toastmaster and have the pleasure of officiating at well over 1000 Royal events, and I have been delighted to know Anne, and to introduce her at top functions in this country and overseas, many of those attended by Britain's Royal Family. I have also engaged her for my clients, in cabaret and she always gave a superb performance.
On one occasion at The Savoy Hotel at a charity ball for The Dockland Settlements, HRH Princess Margaret who was the patron and hostess asked me to invite Anne to her table for

champagne after Anne had completed her cabaret act. But Princess Margaret asked Anne if she would go on stage again and sing her favorite song.

Anne, of course, gave her services to the charity as she did on many occasions, and for many years she was invited to star in a concert for The 'Not Forgotten' Association at Buckingham Palace many of those attending were disabled men and woman from the Second World War. She was also asked to select the artistes for the concert, and I have had the pleasure of being asked by Anne to be the MC, we worked together for many years at the Palace and other places.

One often hears pop stars, after making just one record, referred to as stars and usually some of these stars have a short shelf life, whereas Anne had been in show business for many years and appeared on stage in variety, was a recording artiste and appeared on radio and TV, and of course cabaret. Anne had, apart from a superb voice, great charisma, a lovely personality and great warmth, and I know she is now missed by many people. She was a STAR

ANNE SHELTON *A personal view by* TERESA CAHILL

To most South London families in the post-war years the name of Anne Shelton was little short of iconic. My family was no exception.

At a very early age, I received from older relatives an indelible impression of World War Two and all that it represented. The struggles of the Blitz, the heroism of the armed services, the personal sacrifices and courage of all our people, finally triumphant against all odds and above all the towering inspiration of Sir Winston Churchill were all firmly etched into my subconscious as a child.

The timing of Anne's immediate rise to stardom as a teenager couldn't have been more fortuitous. At a very young age, her amazingly beautiful and mature voice meant that she was immediately taken up by, and permanently associated with, the legendary bandleaders Ambrose and Glenn Miller.

Music was the most important solace in those dark times. Families would gather together around the radio to get the latest news and Anne's performances were an inspiration to all who heard her. Her velvet voice radiated warmth and consolation during the war and afterwards brought nostalgia and patriotism to a new height as people remembered the good experiences and the bad through her songs. For example *Lilli Marlene* which showed that people on both sides of the divide could enjoy the same song, *I'll Be Seeing You,* in which lovers would remember each other always, whether they were fated to see each other again or not and *My Yiddishe Momme* which was particularly poignant at a time when thousands of Jews had somehow survived the Holocaust and were pouring into Britain to start a new life.

This last song was a particular favourite of my mother's, maybe because we had a small amount of Jewish ancestry in the family, way back. Anne's performance had such resonance and passion that I always wondered whether she too, had some Sephardic blood, inherited from her mother's Spanish background.

Thus it was that Anne's place in the history of the Second World War was and still is assured but although she was loved and admired as a great singer by the whole nation for at least fifty years, to the people of South London she was even more special and as a local girl made good, they looked upon her as one of their own.

Imagine the excitement therefore, when my uncle announced with great pride to the rest of the family that Anne Shelton in person had come into his greengrocery shop in Denmark Hill with her family to buy their fruit and vegetables.

At that time, I was growing up in Rotherhithe and in spite of our fairly poor working-class background and having lost my father when I was five, I was encouraged by my sister, brother-in-law and the concert pianist father of a school friend to think of a career in classical music. To help out financially, I took a holiday job in HMV Oxford Street and, with the first money I had ever earned, bought a present for my mother, perhaps to seek her blessing on my ambitions, for she had decided that people from our background who tried to become opera singers would doubtless waste their convent grammar school education and end up in the local pickle factory.

My present to her was Anne's LP *Anne Shelton Showcase* with Wally Stott and his orchestra Philips BBL 7393 which contained the following tracks:

Let's Face The Music And Dance,
Too Young To Go Steady,
Ha!Ha!Ha!,
To Love And Be Loved
Do You Love Me Like You Kiss me
I Got It Bad And That Ain't Good
The Village Of St. Bernadette
The Man That Got Away
Lay Down YourArms
Souvenir d'Italie
Seven Stages Of Man
Smoke Gets In Your Eyes
Perfidia
My Yiddishe Momme

Listening to this record again after years of "bel canto" training, I find Anne's technique quite extraordinary. Basically, she had a low contralto quality but with a very high placement so that if you go to the piano to find out exactly which note she is singing, it is surprising to discover how low the note actually is. This high placement serves her very well in terms of flexibility and enables her to soar upwards and sing high soft notes e.g., in the song *Too Young To Go Steady*, in the second verse, she adds a high note to decorate the word 'me' in the phrase 'treats me like a child', and the effect is amazing. Liquid phrasing and mellifluous tone are there in abundance through every track, though my favourite performances are those where the music demands lyricism and sadness i.e., *I Got It Bad, The Man That Got Away, Smoke Gets In Your Eyes, Too Young To Go Steady* and finally *My Yiddishe Momme*, which is nothing short of an operatic tour de force and which means even more to me now that I have married into a Jewish family. Later on in life, her intonation wasn't always as secure as it had been earlier, but even then, she had an unerring instinct and ability to correct each note if necessary as she sang which always kept her out of vocal trouble. How lucky we are that she made so many fine recordings and that they are all still available so many years later.

In 1960 now aged sixteen, I went with the family on holiday to Dovercourt Bay near Weymouth. When we discovered that Anne was appearing with Morecambe and Wise at the Alexandra Gardens Theatre in a Bernard Delfont variety show called *Showtime* my mother decided that this was a chance not to be missed. None of us had ever heard or seen her perform live and when we did that summer, we were certainly not disappointed. I loved the voice, of course, but what I wasn't expecting was the immense variety of her material and the gigantic, starry personality, which electrified the whole audience but was never egocentric. My mother was not the sort of person confident enough to even consider going round to the stage door, but somehow we found ourselves queuing for Anne's autograph, rather nervously hoping that her offstage persona would not be different from that which we had seen on stage. We needn't have worried; instead of just signing her name, she wrote a long message finishing with "God Bless You" and three kisses. Much later I was to discover that God meant a great deal to her and that we shared a similar Catholic upbringing and half-Irish background.

The years passed and, when I was nineteen and still at music college, my mother died suddenly of a heart attack; I inherited the LP and the programme which I still possess. Having completed my studies, I began my operatic career at Glyndebourne Festival Opera. My debut at Covent Garden followed and from then on, I had a full life singing opera, concerts and recitals all over the world, without having to resort to the pickle factory! I still loved Anne's singing but now that I was a professional myself, whenever I played the records, I appreciated even more her perfect vocal technique.

During a visit to the Dartington Summer School in 1983, where I was giving a Richard Strauss recital. I met the composer Richard Rodney Bennett who became a firm friend. When he needed a friendly attic to store his priceless manuscripts, ours fitted the bill. On one of his visits to the UK, from his home in New York, Richard came for the weekend to look through his papers. Anne Shelton happened to be appearing locally that night at the Lewisham Concert Hall. Richard offered to take me to the show and to introduce me to her afterwards, He had been responsible for the score of John Schlesinger's film *Yanks* and had got to know Anne when she was invited to sing the theme tune for the film- *I'll Be Seeing You.*

What happened next was quite extraordinary. It seemed that night that we had always known each other; there was an instant and amazing rapport and I felt that we would always be friends. An hour later we were still chatting in her dressing room, Richard, Anne, myself and Anne's beautiful sister Jo, who after the death of their mother, had given up her own blossoming singing career to look after that of her sister.

Anne asked if she could have a record of my singing and revealed an enthusiastic knowledge of classical music, particularly the *Cello Concerto* of Edward Elgar, a composer who is very special to me also. A few weeks later, she began a series of radio programmes on Radio 4, in which she chose records of her favourite artists. I tuned in and most unexpectedly, between Bing Crosby, Glenn Miller and Ambrose was a song by Richard Strauss from the record that I had given her. It seemed slightly out of place amongst such greats but I was amazed that she had paid me such a fantastic compliment. A few weeks later I thanked her by agreeing to perform when she asked if I would sing a couple of songs at the 'Not Forgotten' Christmas Lunch in the Royal Mews at Buckingham Palace in December 1984. Ever generous, she had agreed to become Entertainments Officer in charge of the cabaret, which accompanied a Christmas dinner in the winter and a garden party in the summer. Our audience consisted of Navy, Army and Air Force personnel who had been wounded in the service of Queen and Country from the First World War up to the present day.

They were a great audience and seeing their optimism and gallantry one felt honoured to perform for them. On that occasion I met the rest of Anne's family for the first time- husband David, himself ex-Navy and sister Eileen who got on famously with *my* sister Eileen.

Also performing that day was Glenn Miller's brother Herb and the occasion was graced by Katharine, Duchess of Kent whom I came to know better later through her patronage of various musical charities. I remember that the audience were extremely generous to a newcomer and as a result Anne asked me to come again on July 22nd 1986 for the Summer Party. I remember particularly a huge wedding cake, clearly visible through a Palace window as it was the eve of the wedding of Prince Andrew and Sarah Ferguson. It was on that day also that I met Anne's niece Kelly and her partner Di who were to become close friends.

A third invitation to the 'Not Forgotten' Association Summer Party came for me in the following year and on November 5th 1989 the whole family came to lunch at my home. According to Kelly, this occasion was something of a rarity; the family were the closest I had ever come across and it was said that Anne never went out by herself. As a teenage star she was always accompanied by her mother, then later on by one or both of her sisters and also by David, her manager and husband. Consequently, they tended not to visit other people's houses, either separately or together, and kept very much to themselves. Eileen had married and had a family of her own so to a certain extent she had another life away from her siblings but this made no difference in terms of her closeness to the other members of the family.

They arrived, all four of them, in their chauffeur-driven Bentley, at about half past eleven in the morning, for pre-lunch drinks. Anne came clutching a Scottish plaid plastic shopping bag containing all the family jewellery and a present for me, in the form of a cassette tape, which I treasure to this day, of previously unreleased songs by Anne and Jo which they had stayed up late into the previous night to copy for me. Robert and I had assembled our immediate family, all of whom knew Anne's family, through various visits to the 'Not Forgotten' parties at the Palace. David swapped wartime experiences with my brother-in-law Andrew and Robert's father Ian and the girls entertained my sister Eileen and mother-out-of-law Jean with a host of amazing stories. Anne was hysterically funny, could reproduce any accent including Zulu and sang some funny songs, which I couldn't possibly repeat in print. Lunch came and went. Tea came and went. Dinner came and went and they left finally at about three in the morning.

To have the whole family together with mine on that cold day in November was to be an especially poignant memory of an occasion, which was never to be repeated.

On August 5th 1990 Anne was given a dinner at the Berkeley Hotel by the Lady Taverners to celebrate her fifty years in show business and Robert and I were invited to be on the family table. By this time, I was often asked to be the extra sister. Anne, Jo and Eileen was immensely close but had a superstitious fear of being photographed together. Thus, each of them would drop out in turn and I would replace whoever was missing in the photograph. Some people even seemed to think that I looked a little like the other three women and that we could have been from one family.

That night at the Berkeley Hotel, people were already beginning to drift off home when the legendary pianist and bandleader Stanley Black arrived. He was late because, being a Friday night, he had eaten at home first in the usual Jewish tradition. Suddenly he sat down at the piano and began to play. Not to be outdone, Anne started singing and an impromptu performance of star quality ensued. With an audience comprising just a handful of friends and family, Robert and I witnessed two great performers enjoying themselves at the height of their powers. It might well have been the first time that Anne had sung since David's death but her voice was just the same and she knew that she could still produce the goods when necessary.

Later that year she received another important tribute. The day following her birthday was Remembrance Sunday and Anne asked us to come to Baden Powell House where the Frank Sinatra Society would be putting on a celebration in her honour. Records were played, various important performers gave speeches and it struck me then that a great number of people in Britain did not know, perhaps, just how big her international career had been.

Anne was immensely proud of her O.B.E. for services to charity but secretly I always felt that the Establishment had missed the point, perhaps because she never publicised herself for the sake of her own career. I would have liked to see even greater honours heaped upon her for being simply the greatest international singing star that this country has ever produced (our Ella Fitzgerald if you like). As an opera singer, I feel qualified to make this statement. Anne had the natural vocal talent of a Bing, the ease and relaxation of a Perry Como, the imagination and verbal timing of a Sinatra and the passion and dramatic power of a Judy Garland. She could move one to tears with a poignancy that was heart breaking and a few minutes later show all her wit and vivacity in one of the upbeat, chirpy numbers that became popular in the late Fifties. Surely there has never been a singer with such a wide range of vocal colour, such deep artistry, such a perfect vocal technique-and all without a single lesson.

Anne continued to arrange the 'Not Forgotten' garden parties. In the Summer of 1992 when asked, I suggested a Gershwin song but he was not to Anne's liking and thus became the only composer about whom we disagreed. Instead, I was asked to sing the song *When I Grow Too Old To Dream* by Sigmund Romberg. Whether or not Anne thought I could do with some help to wow a rather serious and undemonstrative audience, I don't know, but suddenly she came on to the stage and was at my side singing along an octave beneath me. When I took the tune up an octave higher at the end, to my amazement so did she, finishing on an incredibly high B natural, a long way above her normal range. Afterwards she said that Jo's spirit had come into her mind and urged her to make it a duet. Unfortunately for me, Josie's spirit hadn't thought to enter my mind too so it was all a big surprise to me and to the audience.

In the summer of 1994 I had my 50th birthday, and had planned a big party in the garden. When Anne asked me to sing at the Palace, I felt that I wouldn't have time to practise and so declined. Sadly, it was to be her last.

The party planners arrived in the morning but saw that I had forgotten to buy a floral display for the main table. I went running out of the front door to get something quickly and standing before me was a five-foot high floral arrangement that wouldn't have been out of place at the Savoy. I read the note. Anne was unwell and instead of coming to the party, had sent the flowers to represent her and the family. I was devastated when her niece Kelly kindly rang me the next morning to break the news of her sudden death, before we might have read it in the newspapers.

On her forthcoming birthday, November 10th 1994, we all gathered in Corpus Christi Church, Maiden Lane for a celebration of her life and talent. I remember buying the biggest bunch of British Legion poppies that I could find to put on my coat. Remembering, also, that first meeting with Richard Rodney Bennett and my small Strauss song that she had played on the radio, I chose to sing one of his Four Last Songs. It is called *Beim Schlafengehn*, and is his setting of a poem by Hermann Hesse on the subject of immortality.

Whilst going to Sleep

Now the day has made me tired and my one longing
is for the star-filled night to receive me like a tired child.
Hands, release yourselves from all that you are doing!
Forehead, forget all your thinking!
All of my senses now want to sink into sleep
And the unguarded soul wants to fly and float upwards
to live a thousand times more deeply
in the magic circle of the night.

In July 1997 I was appearing on the radio show *Friday Night Is Music Night* and wanted to sing something in memory of Anne. Richard Rodney Bennett suggested that his colleague, Neil Richardson, might make a new arrangement of *I'll Be Seeing You*.

I felt as though the wheel had come full circle.

The last memory is that of Max Bygraves. He did not appear in the last show with Anne, but he did know her well.

"Anne Shelton was a fun loving, happy-go-lucky gal. Always ready with a smile and a song that was tuneful and well sung. I knew her for about thirty years. Any time we met she would ask 'What's the latest joke Max?' The last time we met was in the middle of Oxford Street, London, when she asked me the same question, I replied 'Anne, I think there is going to be another war' when she asked why? I replied, 'This morning I walked past Vera Lynn's house and I heard her gargling! You could have heard Anne's laughter as far as Marble Arch- I still miss her.

~*~

Well, this is the end of the biography. As my aunt had a career that spanned over sixty years it has been impossible for me to mention every broadcast, show, interview or performance that she ever made as that information is just not available, and even if it were we would need volume two to cover it all.

I hope you have found the factual information of interest and the personal memories enjoyable.

My last words regarding Anne Shelton (Patty) are, "If only all women cared as little as she did about things that don't matter, and as much as she did about things that do."

God Bless you, one and all.

Anne Shelton Discography by Song Titles

With acknowledgements to Geoff Milne of IN TUNE for his discography
1936-1953

Abide With Me DR12702-1 DeE F9005, Lon303, 30135 DeSA FM5885 w.
 Felton Rapley (organ) & The George Mitchell Choir 5/10/48

Absent Friends Philips PB679 USp 544 256-2

Absent Minded Moon R6797 Rex 10129, DeE RFLD.18 Usp 544 267-2 w.
 Jay Wilbur's orch 28/4/42

Adios, My Love PHI PB1165

After You've Gone DLG50549 DeE F9548, Lon.861 w. The All Stars New
 York c October 1950

All Alone with my Shadow DR6205 DeE F7965, BrSA 1986 w. Ambrose &
 his orch 4/9/41

All in the Golden Afternoon DLG50816 Lon.1088, DeEF 9769 w.unknown
 orchestra & chorus NY c9/51

All is Lost DR12518-2 DeE F9180, Lon398, DeSA FM5575 w. The Wardour
 Singers & RR his orch 14/7/48

All My Homeland DR14916 DeE F9428, Lon837 CDEA6081 w. the George
 Mitchell Eight & R.Robertson & his orch 24/4/50

All or Nothing at All DR7449 DeE F8344, RFL.41 Fla PAST CD7048 Peg
 PGN CD821 w. Amb & his orch 29/7/43

Always DR10004 w.S.black & his orch 18/1/46 Unissued

Always in my Heart DR6905 DeE F8183 Emp RAJCD815 w. Ambrose &
 his orch 30/7/42

Amado Mio DR10306 DeE F8635, DeSA FM5193 w. orch cond by Phil
 Green 15/1/46

Amapola DR6060 DeE F7933, DVL.2 RFLD.39 Emp RAJCD815 Fla PAST
 CD7048 Peg PGN CD821 w. Amb & his orch 25/7/41

Amor, Amor DR8422-2 DeE F8430 Castle CD PBX 447/2' w. Amb & his
 orch 9/5/44

And the Angels Sing DR16946 DeE F9932, LF.1106, DFE.6321, ACL.1101,
 RFLD.30, Lon.1224, Lon.LB.707, Ditto DTO.10213 w. Stanley Black
 & his orch 10/4/52

And So I Waited Around DR17026 DEF9941, LF.1106, Lon.LB.707 w.
 Stanley Black & his orch 25/5/52

Angel's Lullaby, The PHI PB994 BBE12347 (SBBE12430)

Anniversary Song DR10874 DeE F8728, DVL.2 544 267-2 Fla PAST CD7850 w. S.Black & his orch 21/11/46

Answer Me OEA 17664-5A HMV B.10596 7M164 MFP 41 1048 3 EMI CDP 7 94763 2 w. The George Mitchell Choir & Orch cond by Frank Cordell 12/10/53

Anywhere DR9537 DeE F8545, RFL.41 w. Amb & his orch 28/6/45

Arrivederci Darling OEA.18478-3B HMV POP 146 MFP 41 1048 3 EMI CBP 7 94763 2 w. Geoff Love & his Orchestra 9/11/55

Asthoreen Dawn DR13772 DeE F9392, Lon1005 w. RR & his orch 23/6/49

As Time Goes By DR 7286 DeE F8307 Castle CD PBX447/2 Voc CDEA6096 w. Amb & his orch 22/4/43

As Time Goes By. PHI BBL7921 WL108 w. Wally Stoftt & his orch.

At Last DR7107 DeE F8247, DVL.2 USp 544 267-2 Fla PAST CD7048 Peg PGN CD821 w. orch acc 11/12/42

At the Cross Roads DR7255 DeE F8295 w. Amb & his orch 12/3/43

Auld Lang Syne For Ever DR17760 DeE F10105 w. the Anne Shelton Singers 2/4/53

Away in a Manger DR12703-1 DeE F9005, Lon303, 30135 w. Felton Rapley (organ) & The George Mitchell Choir 5/10/48

Ay Ay Ay Ay Baio MFP 41 1048 3 As unn. w. orch cond. By Frank Cordell 29/10/54

Ave Marie DR14108 Rejected w. R.Robertson & his och. 30/9/49

Ave Marie DR14263 DeE F9850 Lon580 w. R.Robertson & his orch 4/11/49

Because You Love Me DR12808-2 DeE F9257, Lon382 DeSA FM5761 CDEA608l w. RR & his orch 9/10/48

Because You're Young PHI BBE12292

Begin the Beguine DR4798 DeE F7521, ACL ACL1186, Jas.JASM2017 GKP.9004 Fla PAST CD7048 Castle PBX CD422/2 Peg PGN CD821 w. Ambrose & his Orchestra 7/6/40

Bella Musica DR17104 DeE F9662, Lon.1247 Spec 544 256-2 w. Stanley Black & his orch 4/6/52

Be Mine DR12239-1-2 DeE F8898, Lon239, DeSA FM5575 Voc CDEA6036 w. Roy Robertson & his orch 22/4/48

Beneath the Lights of Home R6063-1 Rex 10029, DeE RFLD.18 USp 544 267-2 w. Jay Wilbur's Orch 30/7/41

Better Not Roll those Blue, Blue Eyes DR7374 DeE F8327 RECDL2 Emp RAJCD815 w. Amb & his orch 19/6/43

Black Eyes DR9482 w. S.Black & his orch 2/6/45 Unissued

Blow, Blow, Winds of the Sea DLG50813 Lon.1088 w unknown orch & chorus new York c 9/51

Blueberry Hill DR5147 DeE F7673 NX 8.120663 ASV CD AJA5150 Voc
  CDEA6096 Peg CDN821 w.Amb & his Orch 4/12/40

Blueberry Hill R5303 Rex9928 w. Jay Wilbur's Orch 2/2/41

Blues in the Night R6880 Rex 10142, DeE DVL.2, BBC CD.608 USp 544
  267-2 Fla PAST CD7048 Peg PGN CD821 w. J.Wilbur's orch 7/7/42

Blue Bahamas DR8112 DeE F8411 w. Amb & his orch 28/1/44

Body and Soul DR16943 DeE F9917, LF.1106, DFE.6321, Lon.1214,
  LB.707 w. S.Black & his orch. 9/4/52

Booglie, Wooglie Piggy, The DR6360 DeE F8011 NX 8.120663 ASV CD
  AJA5150 w. Amb & his orch 21/10/41

Book, The HMV B10641 7M186 MFP41 1048 3 EMI CDP 7 94763 2 w.
  The George Mitchell Choir & orch. Cond. By Frank Cordell 5/1/1954

Boy That Broke My Heart, The. DR10746 DeE F8678 w. Stanley Black
  & his orch 14/8/46

Bridge of Sighs, The OEA.17665-1A HMV B.10596 7M164 MFP 4 1048
  3 CDPB 7 947 2 w. Orchestra cond by Frank Cordell 12/10/53

But Not for Me PHI BBL7289 w. Wally Stott & his orch.

Can't Get Out of this Mood DR7250 DeE F8291 Fla PAST CD7850 w.
  Harry Bidgood & his orch 9/3/43

Can't Help Singing DR9158 DeE F8511 Voc CDEA6096 w. Amb & his
  orch 2/3/45

Carnival is Closed Today, The PHI BF1464 SFMR C5MCS624

Central Park PHI BBL7291 w. Wally Stott & his orch.

Christmas Song, The. DR12517 DeE F8982, Lon304, 30136 w. the Wardour
  Singers & RR & his orch 14/7/48

Christmas Spell, The. DR12504 DEE F8982, Lon304, 30136 PP PPPCD1300
  w. Roy R & his orch 13/1/48

Christmas Star, The 3475 Vista F-476 w the John Alldis Singers Music
  directed by Camarata 45RPM

Come Back Again PHI PB1042 BBE12430 w. Wally Stott orch.

Come Back My Love PHI 326558BF

Come Back to Angouleme DR15775-1 DeE F9622, Lon.935, Lon.LB.707
  CDEA6081 w. the George Mitchell Choir & Bob Farnon & his
  orch. 25/1/51

Coming in on a Wing and a Prayer DR7379-2 DeE F8328, RECDL.2 ASV
  AJA5163 ASV CD AJA5150 Conifer CDHD301 Peg PGN CD821
  ASV PNACD001 RivPro RR CD229/231 w. Amb & his orch 1/7/43

Concerto for Two DR6578-2 DeE F8055 ASV CD AJA5150 Peg PGN
  CD821 w. Amb & his orch (Stanley Black – piano. Les Carew –
  violin) 19/12/41

Constantly DR7106 DeE F8247 w. orch acc. 11/12/42

Continental Waltz, The DR17182 DeE F10001w. Stanley Black & his orch & chorus 17/9/52

Could I Love You More PHI BBE12292

Cross Over the Bridge HMV B10680 7M197 MFP 41 1048 3 EMI CDP 7 9576 2 AS ASCD01 w. Ken Mackintosh & his orch & The Kordettes 11/3/54

Could I Love You More? PHI PB920

Crystal Ball HMV B10628 MFP 41 1048 3 w. orch cond by Frank Cordell 11/12/53

Daddy DR6158 DeE F7953, RFL.41 Emp RAJCD815 Fla PAST CD7048 Castle PBX CD422/2 w. Amb & his orch 21/7/41

Dance with a Dolly DR8892 DeE F8493, RFL.41 w. Amb & his orch 24/11/44

Dancing in the Dark DR9481 DeE IF1023, Lon LPB.59 USp 544 267-2 w. S.Black & his orch 2/6/45

Dancing With Tears In My Eyes PHI BF1302 SFMR 5MCD624

Danny Boy DR8428 w. Stanley Black & his orch Unissued

Danny Boy PHI BF1374 433.635BE PHI431 w. orch accompaniment

Darling DR7342 DeE F8313 w. Amb & his orch 21/5/43

Daydreams AA26239 2H-2 Philips PB616 SFMR 5MCD624 w. Wally Stoff & his Orchestra & Chorus

Dearly Beloved DR7211-2 DeE F8282, RFLD.14 w. Amb & his orch 11/2/43

Dear Old Donegal PHI PHI431 w. orch accompaniment

Do I Love You? DR5623 DeE F7847 w. Amb & his Orch 23/4/1941

Don't Call Me Darling, My Darling DLG50824 Lon.1096 CDEA6081 w. Bernie Landes & his orch New York 17/9/51

Don't Ever Leave Me DR8185 DeE F8416 w. orch cond. By J.Wilbur 17/2/44

Don't Forget PHI PB1110/1165

Don't Get Around Much Anymore DR7381 DeE F8329 w. Amb & his orch 1/7/43

Don't Leave Me Now HMV B10628 MPF 41 1048 3 EMI CDP 7 94763 3 w. orch. Cond. By George Melachrino11/12/53

Don't Misunderstand DR15773-1 DeE F9704, Lon.935 CDEA6081 AS ASCD01 w. Bob Farnon & his orch 25/1/51

Don't Say Goodbye (Auf Wiedersehen) HMV B10857 MFP 41 1048 3 EMI CDP 7 94763 2 w. orch. Cond. By Reg Owen 24/2/55

Don't Worry 'Bout Me PHI BBL7291 w. Wally Stott & his orch.

Do You Love Me Like You Kiss me? PHI PB852 BBE12205 WRC T832 Spec 544 256-2 w. Wally Stott Chorus & orch.

Down at the Old Bull and Bush DR11463-1 DeE F8842, Lon102 w. Harry Roy & his Band 27/7/47

Down by the Glenside DR13773 DeE F9392, Lon1005 2. RR & his orch 23/6/49

Down by the Glenside PHI 433.635BE PHI431 w. orch accompaniment

Down Ev'ry Street R5447 Rex 9954 w. Jay Wilbur's Orch 10/3/41

Dummy Song, The DR17258-1 DeE F10013, Lon.1292 Voc CDLK4198 Spec 544 256-2 w. Ted Heath his Music 17/10/52

Easter Parade (with Bing Crosby) BBC REB.398 AS ASCD01 acc by Jack Russin (piano)

Echo of a Serenade, The. DR8686 DeE F8479 w. S.Black & his orch 6/10/44

End Of The World PHI 326751BF

Eili, Eili DR11461-2 DeE F9196, Lon.103, DeSA FM5772 w. Music by Camarata 27/7/47

Eli, Eli PHI BBE12347(SBBE9003)

Everybody Knew but Me DR10002 DeE F8600 Fla PAST CD7850 w. S.Black & his orch 18/1/46

Ev'ry Night About this Time DR7174-2 DeE F8267, RFLD.14 ASV CD AJA5150 w. Amb & his orch 19/1/43

Ev'rything I Love DR6867-1-2 DeE F8182. Voc CDEA6036 w. Amb & his orch 30/7/42

Ev'ry Time I Look at You DR5307 DeE F7730 w.Amb & his Orch 30/1/41

Festival of Roses DR14917 DeE F9428 w. R.Robertson & his orch 24/4/50

Fine How Do You Do, A. DR7341 DeE F8316 w. orch acc 20/5/43

First Lullaby, The DR5306 DeE F7729 W.Amb & his Orch 30/1/41

Five o'clock Whistle DR5262 DeE F7702 w.Amb & his Orch 17/1/1941

Fools Rush In R.4918 Rex9841, DeE DVL2 Fla PAST CD7048 w. Jay Wilbur's Orch Aug 5,1940

Fools Rush In DR4941, DeE F7580, F7600, BrSA 1784 USp 544 267-2 Emp RAJCD815 NX 8.120663 ASV CD AJA5150 Voc CDEA6096 Peg PGN CD821 w.Amb & his Orch 10/8/40

Fool With a Dream, A. DR7372 DeE F8326 Castle CD PBX447/2 w. Amb & his orch 19/6/43

Forever PHI 6006434 SFMR 5MCD624

Forever and a Day R6064-1 Rex 10029 w. Jay Wilbur's Orch 30/7/41

For Once in Your Life DR11462 Lon.109 w. Roy Robertson & his orch 27/7/47

For You, For Me HMV B10577 MFP41 1048 3 w. orch. Cond. By Frank Cordell 17/9/53

Frenesi DR5472 DeE F7791 2. Ambrose & his orch 14/3/41

Galway Bay DR12359 DeE F8907, Lon287, DeSA FM5547 w. The
Wardour Singers & RR & his orch 24/4/48

Galway Bay PHI 433.636BE PHI431 As unn. w. orch accompaniment

Give Her My Love AA 26257 2H-1 Philips PB661 w. Wally Stott & his
orch & chorus

Give Me Your Hand DR13184-1A DeE F9242, Lon425 w. RR & his orch 2/2/49

Gone Five Minutes DLG50823 Lon.1097 w. Bernie Landes & his orch NY
17/9/51

Go Now DR13034-2 DeE F9283, Lon398 Voc CDA6081 w. RR & his orch
7/12/48

Goodnight Again DR5141DeE F7673 BrSA 1840 w.Amb & his Orch 4/12/40

Good-Night Darling DR10745-1 DeE F8705 Fla PAST CD7850 w. Stanley
Black & his orch. 9/10/46

Good Night, Well it's Time to Go HMV B10745 7M240 MFP 41 1048 3 w.
Ken Mackintosh & his orch. 24/8/54

Goodnight, You Little Rascal, You DR11027 DeE F8772 Fla PAST CD7850
w. Orch cond by Bob Farnon 30/4/47

Great Pretender, The AA 26221 2H-1 Philips PB567 SFMR C5MCD624
Spec 544 256-2 w Wally Stott & his orch & chorus.

Green Eyes DR6333-1 DeE F7992 BrSA 1979 w Sam Browne & Amb & his
orch 8/10/41

Greensleeves DR8023 Lon.287, LPB.59, DeE LF.1023 w. orch cond by
J.Wilbur 7/1/44

Ha! Ha! Ha! PHI PB779 BBE12205 WRC T832 w. Wally Stott his orch &
chorus

Hank Janson Blues DR17845 DeE F10121 w. Johnny Franz & his orch 6/5/53

Happiness is a Thing Called Joe. PHI BBE12169 Wings WL1080 As
Unn. w. Wally Stott & his orch.

Harbour Bells AA 26242 1H-1 Philips PB.641 SFMR 5MCD624 w. Wally
Stott & his orch & chorus

Hearts DR13036 DeE F9102, Lon423 w. RR & his orch 7/12/48

Hearts Don't Lie DR6204 DeE F7965., BrSA 1986 w. Amb & his orch 4/9/41

Heart of Loch Lomond, The DR13187-1 DeE F9100, Lon414, DeSA
FM5886 Voc CDEA6036 w. RR & his orch 2/2/49

He Doesn't Look Much Like a Hero DR7787 DeE F8378 w. Amb & his
orch 25/10/43

He Stole My Heart Away DR6576 DeE F8114, BrSA 2068 2/4/42

Hey! Mabel DR6962-2 DeE F8192 ASV CD AJA5150 w. Amb & his
orch 15/9/42

Hold Back the Dawn DR8022 DeE F8402 w. orch cond by J.Wilbur 7/1/44

Hold Back the Dawn DR17339-1 DeE F10037, SPA.140, Lon.1288 w. acc. Directed by Stanley Black 9/12/52

Hold Me Just a Little Closer Dear DR13475-1 DeE F9148, Lon479 Fla PAST CD7850 Voc CDEA6036 w. PF & his orch 26/4/49

Hollywood Square Dance DR13567 Lon463, DeE RFLD.23 w. Vera Lynn & rhythm acc 11/5/49

Hollywood Square Dance DR13567-3 DeE F9704 w. The Honeycombs 10/6/49

Homeward Bound DR7786 DeE F8378 w. Amb & his orch 25/10/43

Hours I spent with You, The DR13471-1 DeE F9211, Lon479 w. PF & his orch 26/4/49

How About You? DR6755 DeE F8114, RFL.10, BrSA 2068 Emp RAJCD815 w. Sam Brown & Amb & his orch 2/4/42

How Deep is the Ocean? DR10002 RFLD.34, Lon109, LPB59 USp 544 247-2 w. s.Black & his orch 18/1/46

How Did He Look? DR5777 DeE F6771, BrSA 1927 w. Amb & his orch 21/5/41

How Did He Look? Wings WL1080 w. Wally Stoff & his orch.

How Green Was My Valley? DR6804 DeE F8122 Emp RAJCD815 Voc CDEA6096 w. Amb & his orch 1/5/42

How Green Was My Valley? PHI BF1258 SFMR 5MCD624

Humble People DR13470-1 DeE F9153, Lon725 w. Paul Fenoulhet & his orch 26/4/49

Humpty Dumpty Heart DR6859 F8155, RFLD.39 Voc CDEA6096 w. Amb & his orch 4/6/42

Hurry Home PHI PB878 SFMR C5MCD624

I 'Aint Got Nobody DR17846-1 DeE F10121 w. Johnny Franz & his orch 6/5/53

I 'Aint Got Nobody DR17846-2 Unissued w. Rhythm & Trumpet

I 'Aint Got Nobody DR1784603 w. Johnny Franz (Piano) Unissued

I Call Your Name DR13949-1 Lon.831, DeSA FM.5672 w.R.Robertson & his orch 16/8/49

I Can't Love You Anymore (Anymore Than I Do) R.4917 Rex9841, BrSA 1784 w Jay Wilbur's Orch. August 6, 1940

I Cried For You PHI PB1344 w. Johnny Arthur

I'd Like to Set you to Music DR7552-2 DeE F8352 ASV CD AJA5150 w. orch, cond by J.Wilbur 27/8/43

I Don't Mind Being Alone DLG50535 DeE F9548, Lon.850, 30295 w. Jack Pleis & his orch New York c September 1950

I Don't Want to Cry Anymore DR5305 DeE F7729 w. Amb & his Orch
30/1/41

I Don't Want to Set the World on Fire DR6421 DeE F8026, RFLD.14 NX
8.120663 ASV CDAJA5150 w. .Amb & his orch 12/11/41

I Don't Want to Walk Without You DR6803 DeE F8121, F8176 w. Amb &
his orch 1/5/42 Emp RAJCD815

I Don't Want to Walk Without You PHI BF1344
(*Note: F8176 was issued as 'Melody Maker' Competition 1942*)

I Dream of Jeannie With the Light Brown Hair DR8024 w. orch cond. By
J.Wilbur *Unissued*

I Dream of You DR7258 DeE F8296 w. Amb & his orch 12/3/43

I Fall in Love with You Ev'ry Day DR13033 w. RR & his Orch 7/12/48 AS
ASCD01

If I Give my Heart to You HMV B10745 MFP 41 1048 3 EMI CDP 7f 94763
2 w. Ken Macintosh & his orch 24/8/54

If I Were a Blackbird DR15368 DeE F9526, ACL1101, DPA3013 Spec 544
256-2 w the Mayfair orch 9/9/50

If We All Said a Prayer HMV B10857 MFP 41 1048 3 EMI CBP 7 94763 2
w. Orch cond by Reg Owen 24/2/55

If We Met for the First Time DR15508 DeE F9563, Lon.839 w. Dick James
& R.Robertson & his orch 26/11/50

If You Ever Fall in Love Again DR12993 DeE F9100, Lon408 DeSA FM5649
CDEA6081 MFP CD DL-1263 w. The Wardour Singers & RR &
his orch 25/11/48

If You Please DR7448 DeE F8343, RFL.41 Fla PAST CD7048 w. Amb & his
orch 29/7/43

If You've Never Been in Love HMV B10577 MPF 41 1048 3 As unn. w
orch cond by Frank Cordell 17/9/53

I Get Sentimental Over Nothing DR13618-1 DeE F9211, Lon458 Voc
CDEA6036 w. Paul Fenoulhet & his orch 18/5/49

I Get So Lonely (O Baby Mine) HMV B10680 7M197 EMI CDP 7 94763 2
AS unn.

I Give My Heart To You HMV 7M240

I Got it Bad & That 'Aint Good PHI BBL7291 WRC T832 w. Wally Stoff
& his orch.

I Hear that Song Again AA 26292 1H-1 Philips PB.772 SFMR 5MCD624
w. Wally Stott & his orch & chorus

I Just Dropped In to Say Hello DR13185-1A DeE RECD/L.4 Lon.425 w.
Roy Robertson & his orch. 2/2/49

I Just Kissed your Picture Goodnight DR7171 DeE F8266 w. Amb & his orch 19/1/43

I Keep Forgetting to Remember DR11075 DeE F8751, RECD/L.3 MFP CD-DL1263 w. S.B. & his orch 30/1/47

I Know Why DR6484 DeE F8045, RFLD.4, RFL.41 ASV CD AJA5150 w. Amb & his orch 1/12/41

I'll be Near to You AA 26242 2H-1 Philips PB.641 w. Wally Stott & his orch & chorus

I'll Be Seeing You DR8685 DeE F8479, DVL.2 USp 544 247-2 Peg PGN CD821 AS ASCD01 ASV PNACD001 Riv Pro RR CD229/231 ASV CDAJS286 w S.Black & his orch 6/10/44

I'll Be With You in Apple Blossom Time R6644 Rex 10104, DeE DVL.2 2. USp 544 267-2 Fla PAST CD7048 Peg PGN CD821 Jay Wilbur's orch 27/1/42

I'll Dance at your Wedding DR10307 DeE F8635, DeSA FM5193 w. orch cond by Phil Green 5/1/46

I'll Just Close My Eyes R6881 Rex10142, BBC REN.708 w. J.Wilbur's orch 7/7/42

I Just Dropped in to Say Hello DR13185 Lon425, DeE RECD/L.4 w. RR & his orch 2/2/49

I Know Why PHI BBL7291 w. Wally Stott & his orch.

I'll Get By AS ASCD01w. American Band of the Supreme Command cond by Glenn Miller 23/7/44 Broadcast 27/7/44

I'll Never Make the Same Mistake Again DR5076 DeE F7648. RFLD.14 w.Ambrose & his orch 12/11/1940

I'll Never Smile Again DR5011 DeE F7602, DVL.2 Fla PAST CD7048 Peg PGN CD821 w.Ambrose & his Orch 9/9/40

I'll Never Smile Again. PHI BBE12169 Wings WL1080 w. Wally Stott & his orch

I'll Remember Today AA 262922H-2 Philips PB.772 w. Wally Stoff & his orch & chorus

I'll Walk Alone DR8423-2 DeE F8430, RFLD.14, RFL.41 w. Amb & his orch 9/5/44

I'm in a Dancing Mood PHI BBL7291 w. Wally Stott & his orch.

I'm Nobody's Baby R5164 Rex 9903 w. Jay Wilbur's Orch 10/12/40

I'm Praying to St Christopher DR17478 DeE F10061, ACL.1101 w. Stanley Black & his orch 19/1/53

I'm Praying to St Christopher PHI BBE12344

I'm Stepping Out With a Memory Tonight DR5012, DeE F7602 BrSA1794 Peg PGN CD821 w. Ambrose & his Orch 9/9/40

I Never Mention Your Name, Oh No DR7907-2 DeE F8389, DVL.2, RFL.41
Fla PAST CD7048 ASV CD AJA6036 w. Amb & his orch 26/11/43

Inside My Wedding Ring DR6028 DeE F7924 w. Amb & his orch 22/7/41

In The Blue of Evening DR7383 DeE F8330 w. orch acc 5/7/43

In the Chapel of San Remo DR14746 DeE F9393, SPA140, Lon717,
Lon1067 CDEA6081 w. R.Robertson & his orch 13/3/50

In the Middle of a Dance DR6757 DeE F8115, BrSA 2069 2/4/42

In the Still of the Night DR8470 Voc CDEA6036 w. S. Black & his orch
Unissued as 78 6/10/44

I Remember Mama. HMV B10878 MFP41 1048 3 EMI CDP 7 94763 2 w.
chorus & orch cond by Reg Owen 6/5/1955

I Remember the Cornfields DR15301-1 DeE F9477, SPA140, Lon.832,
DeSA FM5761 w. R.Robertson & his orch 28/7/50

I Remember You. PHI BBE12215 Wings WL1080 w. Wally Stott & his orch.

I Shall Return DR17340-1 DeE F10037, ACL.1101, Lon.1288 w. acc directed
by Stanley Black 9/12/52

Isle of Innisfree, The DR17183 DeE F9994, LF.1106, ACL.1101, RFLD.49,
DeSa FM.5981, Lon.LB.107 Spec 544 256-2 w Stanley Black & his
orch 17/9/52

I Spend My Time Remembering R6342-1 Rex 10068 w. Jay Wilbur's orch
10/10/41

I.T.A.L.Y. (I Trust & Love You) Phi PB878

It All Comes Back to Me Now DR10873 DeE F8728 Fla PAST CD7850 w.
Stanley Black & his orch. 21/11/1946

It Always Rains Before the Rainbow R6210 Rex 10040, BrSA 2043, DeE
RFLD.18 544 247-2 w. Jay Wilbur's Orch 5/9/41

It Can't be Wrong DR7905 DeE F8388, RFLD.14, RFL.41 w. Amb & his
orch 26/11/43

It Can't be Wrong PHI BBL7291 w. Wally Stott & his orch.

It Costs So Little DR7086 DeE F7243 w. orch acc

It Could Happen to You DR8849 DeE F8488 w. Amb & his orch 9/11/44

It Happened in Adano DR13469 DeE F9153 CDEA6081CDEA6081 w.
Paul Fenoulhet & his orch 26/4/49

It's a Marshmallow World DR13950 DeE F9552, Lon.539 w. R.Robertson
& his orch. 16/8/49

It's a Small World DR6423 DeE F7027 NX 8.120663 Voc CDEA6096 w.
Ambrose & his orch 12/11/41

It's You PHI PB1215 SFMR 5MCD624w. Wally Stott & his orch.

It's You that I Love DR7371 DeE F8326 w. Amb & his orch 19/6/43

I Talk to the Trees DR17759 DeE F10105, Acl.1101, RFLD.49 Spec 544 256-2 w. Harry Grove & his orch 2/4/53

I Understand DR5897 DeE F7902 w. Amb & his orch 18/6/41

I Understand PHI 326530BF

I Want My Mama DR5553 DeE F7828, BrSA 1903 w. Amb & his Orch 4/4/41

I Will Light a Candle PHI1110

It Won't Be Long 'Til Christmas 3474 Vista F-476 w The John Alldis Singers music directed by Camarata 45RPM

I Will Never Change DR15929 DeE F9664, Lon.1052 w. The George Mitchell Choir & Robert Farnon & his orch 12/1/51

Johnny Bach DR13467 DeE F9180, Lon479 w. The Wardour Singers & Paul Fenoulhet & his orch 26/4/49

Johnny Fiddler (I Got) DR5304 DeE F7729, BrSA 1872 2.Amb & his Orch 30/1/41

Johnny Get Your Girl DR12990 DeE F9056, Lon408 w. The Keynotes & RR & his orch 25/11/48

Johnny Zero DR7380 DeE F8329, RFLD.4 w. Amb & his orch 1/7/43

Journey's End DR8320 DeE F8421, RFL.41 w. Amb & his orch 31/3/44

Juke Box Rag OEA19003-5B HMV B10732 MFP 41 1048 3 w Orchestra conducted by Geoff Love 11/6/54

Just Look Around (Words by Jo Shelton) no further details ?

Just Love Me Phi PB920 BBE12292

Kiss in the Dark, A. DR12807-1 DeE F9257, LF1023, Lon382 30135 DeSA FM5885 CDEA6081 w. The Wardour Singers & Roy Robertson & his orch 9/10/48

Kiss of Fire DR16945 DeE F9917, LF.1106, DFE.6321, ACL.1101, Lon.1234, LB.707 Spec 544 256-2 w. Stanley Black & his orch 10/4/52

Kissing Tree, The HMV B10547 MFP 41 1048 3 EMI CDP 7 94763 2 w. orch cond by George Melachrino 30/8/53

Kiss the Boys Goodbye DR6422 DeE F8026, RFLD.4 USp 544 267-2* 544 427-2* Conifer CDHD301 Castle PBX CD447/2 Peg PGN CD821 w. Amb & his orch. 12/11/41

Kiss the Boys Goodbye R6529-1 Rex 10089, DeE DVL.2 Fla PAST CD7048 w. Jay Wilbur's orch 8/12/41

Kiss Me Goodnight DR12992-1-2 DeE F9056, Lon373 DeSA FM5611 Voc CDEA6036 w. The Wardour Singers & Roy Robertson & his orch 25/11/48

Lady Who Didn't Believe in Love, The. DR7344 DeE F8314, RFL.41 Fla PAST CD7048 w. Amb & his orch 21/5/43

Land of Sunshine DR15367 DeE F9537, DeSA, FM.5723 w. the Mayfair orch 9/9/50

Last Time I Saw Paris, The R5448 Rex 9954, DeE DVL.2 2. USp 544 267-2 Fla PAST CD7048 Peg PGN CD821 Jay Wilbur's Orch 10/3/41

Laura DR9483-2 DeE F8538 Emp RAJCD875 Fla PAST CD7850 w. S.Black & his orch 2/6/45

Law is Comin' Fer Ya, Paw, The DR12369-2 DeE F8963, Lon260 CDEA6081 w Sam Browne & The Keynotes w orch accompaniment 28/5/48
Note: The recording card shows the above title as by Elsie Loo & Sturdy Bo Bronson with The Panhandle Boys!

Lay Down Your Arms AA 26239 1H-1 Philips PB616 BBE12090 WRC T832 SFMR 5MCD624 Spec 544 256-2 As unn. w. Wally Stott & his Orchestra & Chorus

Let Me This Day DR17479 DeE F10061 w. Stanley Black & his orch 19/1/53

Let there be Love DR5773 DeE F7876, RFL10 Emp RAJCD815 w. Sam Browne & Amb & his Orch 22/5/41

Let there be Love. Wings W1080 w. Wally Stott & his orch.

Let's Face the Music & Dance PHI BBL7291 WRC T832 w. Wally Stott & his orch.

Let's Harmonise DR13566 Lon463, DeE RFLD.23 CDEA6081 w. Vera Lynn & rhythm acc 11/5/49

Let's Keep it that Way DR9807-1 DeE F8588/F41007 RECD/L.3 w. S.Black & his orch 12./11/45

Life is Nothing Without Music DR8748 DeE F8592 w. Amb & his orch 23/11/45

Lights Out Until Reveille DR6359 DeE F8010, BrSA 1977 w. Amb & his orch 21/10/41

Lilli Marlene DR8426-2 DeE F8434, RECD/L.3, RFLD.18, Lon.144 USp 544 267-2 EMP RAJCD845 Voc CDEA6036 ASV CD AJA5150 Peg PGN CD821 RivPro RR CD229/331 w. Stanley Black & his orch 10/5/44

Lilli Marlene's Lullaby DR16944 DeE F9932, Lon.1224 w. Stanley Black & his orch 9/4/52

Little Drops of Water DR17199-1 DeE F9994, DeSa FM.5981, Lon.1264 CDEA5081 w. Acc directed by Harry Grove 18/9/52

Little Love, a Little Kiss, A DR14107 Lon.539 w. R.Robertson & his orch 30/9/49

Little Steeple Pointing to a Star, A DR5625 DeE F7848 Emp RAJCD815 Voc CDEA6108 w. Amb & his orch 23/4/41

Little Town in the Ould County Down PHI PHI431 w. orch accompaniment

Loch Lomond DR8429 w. Stanley Black & his orch. Unissued

Love at Last R5904 Rex 10007 w. Jay Wilbur's Orch 19/6/41

Love, Here is my Heart DR8851 DeE F8488 w. Amb & his orch 9/11/44

Love Him So much I could Scream OEA18002-4B HMV B.10732 MFP 41 1048 3 AS unn. w Orchestra cond by Geoff Love 11/6/54

Love is a Song DR7032 DeE F8221 w. orchestral accompaniment 14/10/42

Loveliest Night of the Year, The DR15782-1 DeE F9692, LF.1106, ACL.1101, Lon.937, LB.707 Spec 544 256-2 w. The George Mitchell Choir & Robert Farnon & his orch. 25/1/51

Love Me, My Love DR15781-1 DeE F9622, Lon.937 CDEA6081 w. the George Mitchell Choir & Bob Farnon & his Orchestra 25/1/51

Love of my Life DR11845-1 DeE F8951, SPA140, Lon198 MFP CD-L 1269 Fla PAST CD7850 w. Orch dir by Camarata 30/11/47

Lover Man (Oh Where Can You Be) DR11464-1 DeE F8842, SPA.140, RFL.20, Lon102 Voc CDEA6081 Fla PAST CD7850 w. Harry Roy & his Band 27/7/47

Lover's Waltz, The DR15783 Lon.936 w. Dick James & Paul Dallas & his orch 25/1/51

Love Time DLG50815 Lon.10897 w. unknown orchestra & chorus New York c9/51

Mademoiselle de Paris DR15928 DeE F9664, Lon.1067 w. The George Mitchell Choir & Robert Farnon & his orch 12/1/51

Madonna in Blue, The AA 26227 2H-1 Philips PB.437 BBE12090 BBE12234 w. Wally Stoff & his orch & chorus.

Maizy Doats and Dozy Doats DR8319 DeE F8422 Castle CD PBX 447/2 w. Amb & his orch 31/3/44

Mañana DR9847 DeE F8580 w. Amb & his orch 23/11/45

Man on the March, AA 26257 1H-1 Philips PB661 w. Wally Stott his orch & chorus

Man That Got Away, The PHI BBL7291 WRC T832 w. Wally Stott & his orch.

Maybe DR5146 DeE F7671 NX 8.120663 w.Amb & his Orch 4/12/40

Maybe R5165 Rex 9903 w. Jay Wilbur's Orch 10/12/40

Melancholy Minstrel DR12505 DeE F9231, Lon267 Fla PAST CD7850 w. RR & his Orch 13/7/48

Merry Christmas DR15300 DeE F9551 Lon.837 Voc CDLK4199 w. RR & his orch 28/7/50

Minnie from Trinidad Dr6068 DeE F7934, BrSA 1970 Emp w. Amb & his orch 30/7/41

Moaning Minnie OEA-2675-1 HMV BD5024, Saville.SVL.158 (as Pat Sibley) w. Jack Hylton's Orchestra dir. Billy Ternant January 19, 1936

Moon for Sale DR5200DeE F7694 w.Amb & his Orch 30/12/40

Moonlight in Mexico DR6062 DeE F7936. BrSA 1970 NX 8.120663 w. Amb & his orch 25/7/41

More and More DR9159 DeE F8511, RECDL.2 Voc CDEA6096 w. Amb & his orch 2/3/45

More than Anything Else in the World DR10528 DeE F8678 w. S.Black & his orch 9/10/46

Moth and the Flame, The DR17388 DeE F10048 Spec 544 256-2 w. Edmundo Ros & his orch 18/12/52

Mountains of Mourne, The 433.636BE PHI PHI431 w. orch accompaniment

Music by the Angels DLG50534 DeE F9593, Lon.852, 30295 w. Jack Pleis & his orch New York c 9/50

Music, Music, Music DR14747 DeE F9393 CDEA6081 w. Rhythm Accompaniment 13/3/50

My Beautiful Sarie Marais DR9042-2 DeE F8510, DeSA FM5723, DEIrl W5040 w. S.Black & his orch 15/1/45

My Christmas Wish DR15299 DeE F9551, Lon.837 Voc CDLK4199 w. R.Robertson & his orch 28/7/50

My Concerto DLG50821 Lon.1096, DeE F9850 CDEA6081 w. Bernie Landis & his orch New York 17/9/51

My Continental Love PHI 326571BF

My Devotion DR7104 DeE F8246 Emp RAJCD815 w.Amb & his orch 10/12/42

My Gypsy Heart HMV 7M279

My Heart Sings. PHI BBE12169 Wings WL1080 w. Wally Stott & his orch.

My Love Loves Me DR13579-1A DeE F9477, Lon532, DeSA FM5672 w. & PF & his orch 13/5/49

My One & Only Love PHI 6006434 SFMR 5MCD624

My Serenade DR7074 DeE F8242 Voc CDEA6096 w. Amb & his orch 11/11/42

My Silent Love DR11835-2 DeE F8974, LF1023, SPA140, Lon118, LPB59 Fla PAST CD7850 Voc CDEA6036 w orch dir by Camarata 28/11/47

My Yiddishe Momme DR5791-2 DeE F7891, RFL41, BrSA 1928 Emp RAJCD815 USp 544 267-2 ASV CD AJA5150 Peg PGN CD821 w. Amb & his orch 22/5/41

My Yiddishe Momme DR11467-1 DeE F9197, SPA140, Lon103, DeSA FM5772 w. Music by Camarata 28/7/47

My Yiddishe Momme PHI BBE12437(SBBE9003) WRC T832 w. Wally Stott & his orch.

Nain, Nain DR7256 DeE F8295, RFLD.39 w. Amb & his orch 12/3/43

Nein, Nein Fraulein PHI PB1215 SFMR 5MCD624

Night and Day DR8471 DeE LF.1023, Lon.LPB.59 Voc CDEA6036 w.
  S.Black & his orch 6/10/44

Night Has a Thousand Eyes, The. DR11842-2 DeE F8926, SPA140, Lon.210
  Fla PAST CD7850 Voc CDEA6036 w. orch dir by Camarata 30/11/47

Nightingale DR7073-2 DeE F8242 ASV CD AJA5150 w. Amb & his orch
  11/11/42

Nightingale Sang in Berkeley Square, A DR4819 DeE F7539, DeA 3469.
  BrSA1803, DeE DVL.2 NX 8.120663 Fla PAST CD7048 Peg PGN
  CD821 w.Ambrose & his Orchestra June 25, 1940

Not Anymore DR8021 DeE F8402 w. orch cond. By J.Wilbur DeE F8402 7/1/44

Now Hear This AA326377-IF PHI PB956 AA326377IF SFMR C5MCD

Now I Know Wings WL1080 w. Wally Stoff & his orch

October Twilight DR12234 DeE F8950, Lon236 w. Roy Robertson & his
  orch 21/4/48

O Baby, I Get So Lonely HMV 7M197

Oh, Baby Mine I Get So Lonely MFP 41 1048 3 w. Ken Mackintosh & his
  orch. 11/3/1954

Oh! Baby, What Can I Do? DR14422 Lon.30092 w. the Keynotes & the
  David Reid Quintet 20/12/49

Oh! Baby, What Can I Do? DR14490-1A Lon.645 w. the Keynotes and
  the David Reid Quintet 16/1/50

Oh! Buddy, I'm in Love F5268 DeE F7705, BrSA1872 w.Amb & his Orch
  17/1/41

Oh! My Darling DR11843-1-2 DeE F9327, Lon198 Voc CDEA6036 MFP
  CD-DL1263 w. orch dir by Camarata 30/11/47

Once in a While DR15365-1 DeE F9526, Lon.832 w. Orchestral
  Accompaniment 9/9/50

Only a Moment Ago DR15366-1 DeE F9537, Lon.831 w. Orchestral
  Accompaniment 9/9/50

Only Forever DR5357 DeF7741 NX 8.120663 ASV CD AJA5150 Peg PGN
  CD821 w. Amb & his orch 14/2/41

Only You DR7012 DeE F8214 Emp RAJCD815 w. Amb & his orch 7/10/42

On the Aitchison, Topeka and the Santa Fe DR9848-1 DeE F8579 Voc
  CDEA6036 w. Amb & his orch 23/11/45

On the Painted Desert DR12235 DeE F8950, Lon 236 Fla PAST CD7850
  w. Roy Robertson & his orch 21/4/48

One Night in Old Seville DR10746-1 DeE F8705 w. Orch Acc. Conducted
  by S.Black 9/10/46

Our Love Affair DR5358 DeE F7741, BrSA 12882 NX 8.120663 w.Ambrose
  & his Orchestra 14/2/1941

Out of the Night DR9806 DeE F8588 Fla PAST CD7850 w. Stanley Black
  & his orch 12/11/45

Pablo the Dreamer DR9484-2 DeE F8538/F41007, DeSA Fm5193 Emp
  RAJCD875 w. S.Black & his orch 2/6/45

Pair of Silver Wings, A R5692 Rex 9984, DeE DVL.2 Fla PAST CD7048 w.
  Jay Wilbur's Orch 8/5/41

Pair of Silver Wings, A DR5776 DeE F7877, BrSA 1927 USp 544 267-2*
  ASV CD AJA5150 w. Amb & his Orch 21/5/41

Papa Loves Mama PHI PB1042 BBE12430 w. Wally Stott orch.

Paper Doll DR8027 DeE F8398 w. Amb & his orch 7/1/44

Perfidia WRC T832 AS unn. w. Wally Stott & his orch.

Petite Waltz DR15507 DeE F9563, Lon.839 w. Dick James, Anton Karas
  (Zither) & Roy Robertson & his orchestra 26/11/50

Porgy PHI BBL7291 w. Wally Stott & his orch.

Put Your Arms Around Me Honey DR7555 DeE F8351 w. Amb & his orch
  27/8/43

Put Your Shoes on Lucy DR13186 w. The Keynotes & RR & his Orch 2/
  2/49 *Rejected*

Put Your Shoes on Lucy DR13192 DeE F9102, Lon414 DeSA Fm5611
  Spec 544 256-2 w. The Keynotes & rhythm acc.3/2/49

Question and Answer DR7208-2 DeE F8279 w. orch acc 10/2/43

Rainy Night in Rio, A. DR11206 DeE F8772 Fla PAST CD7850 w. Orch
  cond by Bob Farnon 30/4/47

Ring Around the Moon DR12236-1 DeE F9203, Lon309 w. Ted Heath &
  his music 22/4/48

Robin Hood DR9538 DeE F8546, RFL.41 w. Amb & his orch 28/6/45

Rockabye Ranch DR13617 Lon532 w. Paul Fenoulhet & his orch 18/5/49

Rome PHI 326530BF

Room Five-Hundred-and-Four DR5360 DeE F7742 Voc CDEA6072 w.
  Ambrose & his Orch. 14/2/41

Rose of Santa Luzia DR10001 DeE F8600 Fla PAST CD7850 w. S.Black &
  his orch 18/1/46

Rose of Tralee PHI 433.636BE PHI431 w. orch accompaniment

Russian Rose DR6069 DeE F7935 Emp RAJCD815 w. Amb & his orch 30/7/41

Sail Along Silv'ry Moon PHI PB815 SFMR 5MCD624

Sailor PH PB1096 BBE12430 Spec 544 256-2 AS unn. w. Wally Stott & his
  orch.

Sand in My Shoes PHI BBL7291 w. Wally Stott & his orch.

San Fernando Valley DR8598-2 DeE F8465 Voc CDEA6036 w. Amb & his
  orch 27/7/44

Santa Maria Dr17105 DeE F9962, ACL.1101, Lon.1247 w. Stanley Black & his orch 4/6/52

Say Something Sweet to Your Sweetheart DR12370-1 DeE F8963, Lon260 Voc CDEA6081 w. Sam Browne & The Keynotes w. orchestral accom. 28/5/48 Note The recording card shows the above title as by Elsie Loo & Sturdy Bo Bronson with The Panhandle Boys!

Seems Like Yesterday DR14745-1 Lon.725 w. R.Robertson & his orch 13/3/50

September Song. PHI BBE12218 Wings WL1080 w. Wally Stott & his orch.

Serenade "Frasquita" DR9353 DeE F8545 w. Amb & his orch 28/6/45

Seven Days AA 26221 1H-1 Philips PB567 BBE12090 Spec 544 256-2 w. Wally Stott & his orch & chorus

Seven Stages of Man Philips PB679 WRC T832 w. Wally Stott & his orch.

Siberia AS ASCD01 (No further details?) *previously unissued?*

Silver Wings in the Moonlight DR7553-2 DeE F8352 ASV CD AJA5150 w. orch cond by J.Wilbur 27/8/43

Sing me a Song of the Islands DR6907 DeE F8184 w. Amb & his orch 30/7/42

Slow, Slow Winds of the Sea

Smoke Gets in your Eyes. Wings PHI BBE12169 WL1080 WRC T832 w. Wally Stott & his orch.

Softly Beat the Drum PHI BF1374

So Long Sarah Jane DR7686 DeE F8358, RFL.41 Fla PAST CD7048 w. Amb & his orch 24/9/43

Someday Soon DR8028 DeE F8398 w. Amb & his orch 7/1/44

Some of These Days DLG50548 DeE F9593, Lon.861 w. The All Stars New York c. Oct 1950

Some Other Time DR8850 DeE F8498 w. Amb & his orch 9/11/44

Some Sunny Day R6645 Rex 10104 2. Jay Wilbur's orch 27/1/42

Something to Remember You By DR5401 DeE F7772, DeA 18358 NX 8.120663 w. Ambrose & his Orch 27/2/41

Somewhere Over the Hill DR7214 DeE F8283 w. Amb & his orch 11/2/43

Song of the Barefoot Contessa (My Gypsy Heart) HMV B10789 7M279 MFP41 1048 3 EMI CDP7 94763 2 w. orch cond by Frank Cordell 29/10/54

Song of The Trees OEA18479-4B HMV POP.146 MFP41 1048 3 w. Geoff Love & his Orchestra 9/11/55

Sound of Summer, The PHI BF1464

South Wind DR7013 De E F8214 Emp RAJCD815 w. Amb & his orch 7/10/42

Souvenir dee Paree DR12360 DeE F8964, Lon423 w. RR & his orch 24/4/48

Souvenir d'Italie AA 26280 2H-1 Philips PB.726 BBE12205 WRC T832 SFMR C5CD624 w. Wally Stott & his orch & chorus

Souvenir of Ireland PHI PB1096 BBE12430 PHI431 w Wally Stott & his orch.

Spring in December DR11846 DeE F8974, Lon158 Voc CDEA6081 Fla PAST CD7850 w. orch dir by Camarata 30/11/47

Spring Will be a Little Late this Year DR8671 DeE F8480 w. Amb & his orch 9/8/44

St Mary's in the Twilight R6211 Rex 10040, BrSA 2943 w. Jay Wilbur's orch 5/9/41

St Louis Blues DR5792 DeE F7892, BrSA 1929 Emp RAJCD815 NX 8.120663 w. Amb & his orch 22/5/41

Stormy Weather DR5780 BrSA 1928…reserved for DeE F7979 but not issued. W. Amb & his Orch 21/5/41

Strange as it Seems DR6857 DeE F8156 w. Amb & his orch 4/6/42

Strangers in the Dark DR11844 DeE F8926, RECD/L.3, Lon158 Voc CDEA6081 Fla PAST CD7850 w orch dir by Camarata 30/11/47

Swinging on a Star-2 DR8670 DeE F8476 ASV CD AJA 5150 Voc CDEA6096 Peg PGN CD821 w. Amb & his orch 9/8/44

Symphony of Spring DR14307 Lon.579 CDEA6081 w. Rhythm accompaniment 18/11/49

Take a Chance DR17389 DeE F.10048 w. Edmundo Ros & his Orch 18/12/52

Take Care of Love DR14308-1A DeE F9552 Lon.579 w. Roy Robertson & His Orchestra 18/11/49

Take it Easy DR8113 DeE F8411 w. Amb & his orch 28/1/44

Take it from There DR7554 DeE F8351 w. Amb & his orch 27/8/43

Take Off the Coat DR15776 Lon.936 AS ASCD01 w. The Paul Dallas Five 25/1/51

Taking a Chance on Love DR7345 DeE F8313, RFLD,4 RFL.41 Fla PAST CD7048 Peg PGN CD821 w. Amb & his orch 21/5/43

Taking a Chance on Love. PHI BBE12218 Wings W11080 w. Wally Stott & his orch.

Tangerine. PHI BBE12218 Wings WL1080 w. Wally Stott & his orch.

Taxi Driver's Serenade, A. DR7103 DeE F8245 Emp RAJCD815 w. Amb & his orch 10/12/42

Teach Me Tonight HMV B10789 7M279 MFP 41 1048 3 EMI CDBP 7 94763 2 w. Geoff Love & his orch. 28/10/54

Tell Me Again In The Morning PHI 326558BF

Tenement Symphony - Pt 1 DR8025 DeE F8397, Lon335 Voc CDEA6036 ASV CD AJA5150 w. Amb & his orch 7/1/44

Tenement Symphony - Pt 2 DR8026 DeE F8397, Lon335 Voc CDEA6036 ASV CD AJA5150 Peg PGN CD821 w. Amb & his orch 7/1/44

Thanks for the Dream DR8184 DeE F8416 w. orch cond by Jay Wilbur 1/2/44

Thanks to You DR13616-1 Lon 473 w. Paul Fenoulhet & his orch 18/5/49

That Lovely Weekend DR6525 DeE F8047, RFL.10 Voc CDEA6072 w. Amb & his orch 4/12/41

That's an Irish Lullaby DR9043-2 DeE F8510, DeIrl W5040 w. S.Black & his orch 15/1/45

That's an Irish Lullaby PHI 433.635BE

That's the Chance You Take Dr17027 DeE F9941, ACL.1101 w. Stanley Black & his orch 25/5/52

That's the Moon, My Son DR7207-2 DeE F8279, RECD/L.3 USp 544 267-2 w. orch acc 10/2/43

There are Such Things DR7249 DeE F8291 Fla PAST CD7850 w. Harry Bidgood & his orch 9/3/43

There Goes that Song Again DR5898 DeE F7902 Fla PAST CD7048** w. Amb & his orch 18/6/41

There Goes that Song Again R5901 Rex 10007 w. Jay Wilbur's orch 19/6/41

There's a Harbour of Dream Boats DR7285 DeE F8306 Voc CDEA6096 w. Amb & his orch 12/4/43

There's a Land of Begin Again DR6482 DeE F8044 w. Amb & his orch 1/12/41

There's a Lull in my Life. Wings WL1080 w. Wally Stott & his orch.

There's a New Moon Over the Ocean DR11076 DeE F8751, RECD/L.3 w. SB 7 his orch 30/1/47

There's no Song Like an Irish Song PHI 433.635BE PHI431 w. orch accompaniment

They Met in Rio DR5900 DeE F7902 w. Sam Browne & Amb & his orch 18/6/41

Things I Love, The Dr6026 DeE F7923 w. Amb & his orch 22/7/41

This is No Laughing Matter R6796 Rex 10129 w. Jay Wilbur's orch 28/4/42

This is the Time of the Year DLG50822 Lon.1097CDEA6081 w. Bernie Landes & his orch NY 17/9/51

Three Roads AA 26280 1H-1 Philips PB.726 w. Wally Stott & his orch & chorus

Till the Stars Forget to Shine DR8597 DeE F8465 w. Amb & his orch 27/7/44

Time May Change DR12238 DeE F8898, Lon255 CDEA6081 AS ASCD01 w. Roy Robertson & his orch 22/4/48

Time Out for Tears-1-2-3 DR12358 DeE F8964, Lon239 Voc CDEA6036 w. The Keynotes & RR & his orch 24/5/48

Tobermory Bay HMV B10547 MFP 41 1048 3 EMI CDP 7 94763 2 w. orch cond. By George Melachrino 30/8/53

Tomorrow's Sunshine DR6749 DeE F8113 2. Emp RAJCD815 w.Amb & his orch 31/3/42

Tonight I kissed You DR8427-2 DeE F8343 Emp RAJCD845 Voc CDEA6036 w. S.Black & his orch 10/5/44

Tonight's My Night PHI BF1302 SFMR 5MCD624

To Love & be Loved PHI AA326377-2F WRC T832 As unn w. Wally Stott & his orch.

Too-Ra-Loo-Ra-Loo-Ra (That's an Irish Lullaby) PHI PHI431 w. orch accompaniment

Too Young to Go Steady AA 26277 1H-2 Philips PB.437 BBE12090 WRCT832 SFMR C5MCD624 Spec 544 256-2 w Wally Stott & his orchestra

Tread Softly (You're Stepping On My Heart) PHI BBE12292 SFMR 5MCD624

Tread Softly AS unn (Special dubbing AS and Jo Shelton sing a duet from record above)

Trolley Song, The. DR88891 DeE F8498 w. Amb & his orch 24/11/44

Twilight DR13578-2 DeE F9231, SPA140, Lon458 Voc CDEA6036 w. The GM Choir & PF & his orch 13/5/49

Until They Sail PHI PB779

Until You Fall in Love DR5078 DeE F7649 EMP RAJCD815 Voc CDEA6072 w.Ambrose & his orch 12/11/40

Velvet Touch, The. DR12516 DeE F9283, Lon267Fla PAST CD7850 w. The Wardour Sings & RR & his orch 14/7/48

Very Thought of You, The. DR9041 DeE LF.1023, Lon LPB59 w. S.Black & his orch 15/1/45

Village of St Bernadette PHI PB969 BBE12344 WRC T832 SFMR 5MCD624 Spec 544 256-2 AS ASCD01 w. Wally Stott & his orch.

Volare PHI PB825, BBE12205 SFMR C5MCD624 Spec 544 256-2 w. Wally Stott his orch & chorus.

Wallflower Waltz, The DR17200-1 DeE F10013, Lon.1264 w. acc directed by Harry Grove18/9/52

Waltzing in the Clouds DR5359 DeE F7742 w Ambrose & his orch 14/2/41

Wedding of Lilli Marlene, The DR13468-1-2A DeE F9148, Lon477 DeSA FM5611 Fla PAST CD7850 Voc CDEA6036 w. The Wardour Singers & Paul Fenoulhet & his orch 26/4/49

Wedding Waltz The DR9536 DeE F8546, RFL.41 w. Amb & his orch 28/6/45

We Mustn't Say Goodbye DR7684-2 DeE F8358 ASV CD AJA5150 w. Amb & his orch 24/9/43

We Three (My Echo, My Shadow & Me) DR5265 DeE F7703 NX 8.120663 ASV CD AJA5150 Voc CDEA6096 w.Amb & his Orch 17/1/41

What Did I Do? DR12237-1 DeE F9203, London309 w. Ted Heath & his music 22/4/48

What Have They Told You HMV B10878 MFP 41 1048 3 w. chorus & orch cond. By Reg Owen 6/5/55

What'll I Do? DR11915-3 DeE F8859, Lon210 Voc CDEA6036 w. orch dir by Camarata 29/12/47

When I Look at You DR7382 DeE F8330 w. orch acc. 5/7/43

When Irish Eyes are Smiling PHI PHI431 w. orch.acc.

When the Heather Gleams Like Stardust DR14264 DeE F9342 Lon.580 CDEA6081 w. R.Robertson & his orch 4/11/49

When Night is Thru' DR6579 DeE F8055 w. Amb & his orch 19/12/41

When that Man is Dead and Gone DR5471 DeE F7791, BrSA 1906 w. Ambrose & his Orch 14/3/41

When the Lilac Blooms Again DR'12991 DeE F9076 w. RR & his orch 25/11/48

Where Can I Go PHI PB994 BBE12347(SBBE9003) SFMR C5MCD624

Where Flamingos Fly DR11847-2 DeE F8859, SPA140, Lon210 Fla PAST CD7850 Voc CDEA6036 w. orch dir by Camarata 30/11/47

Where in the World DR6906-2 DeE F8184, RFLD.14 Voc CDEA6036 ASV CD AJA5150 Peg PGN CD821 w. Amb & his orch 30/7/42

Where's My Love DR7343 DeE F8314, RFLD.14 Fla PAST CD7048 w. Amb & his orch 21/5/43

Where or When DR9040 DeE LF1023, DVL.2, Lon.255, Lon. LPB59 USp 544 267-2 Voc CDEA6036 w. S.Black & his orch 15/1/45

Where Were You When I Needed You? PHI BF1258 SFMR 5MCD624

While the Angelus Was Ringing DR13035-1 DeE F9076, SPA140, Lon373, DeSA FM5586 w. The Wardour Singers & Roy Robertson & his orch 7/12/48

While the Music Plays On DR6334 DeE F7993, BrSA 1978 Emp RAJCD815 Castle PBX CD422/2 Flare ROYCD239 w. Amb & his orch DR6334 8/10/41

White Christmas DR6980 DeE F8193 w. Amb & his orch 13/7/42

Who am I? R5651 Rex 9984 w. Jay Wilbur's Orch 8/5/41

Whose Girl Are You? DR13577-1 Lon473 w. Paul Fenoulhet & his orch 3/5/49

Why Can't it Happen to Me? DR7085 DeE F8243 w. orch acc. 11/11/42

Why Did She Fall for the Leader of the Band? OEA-2676-1-2 HMV BD5023 (as Pat Sibley) w Jack Hylton's Orchestra dir. Billy Ternant January 19, 1936

Why Does it Have to be Me? HMV B10641 7M186 MFP 41 1048 3 w. The
George Mitchell Choi & orch cond. By Frank Cordell 5/1/54

Why Don't You Fall in Love with Me? DR7284 DeE F8306 Voc CDEA6096
w. Amb & his orch 22/4/43

With my Shillelagh under my Arm PHI PHI431 AS unn. w. orch
accompaniment

Without That Certain Thing DR14491-1A DeE F9327, Lon.645, 30092 w.
the Keynotes & the David Reid Quintet 16/1/50

Without That Certain Thing DR14491 Lon.645 w. the Keynotes & the
David Reid Quintet 16/1/50

Wonderful One DR17257-1 DeE F10013, LF.1106, ACL.1101, DFE.6321,
Lon.1292, Lon.LB.707 Voc CDLK4198 w. Ted Heath & his Music
17/10/52

Woody Woodpecker, The DR12503 DeE F8951 w. The Keynotes & Roy
Robertson & his orch 13/7/48

World is Mine Tonight, The DLG50814 Lon.1087, DeE F9769, ACL.1101
w. unknown orchestra & chorus New York c 9/51

Wrap Yourself in Cotton Wool R6530-1 Rex 10089 w. Jay Wilbur's orch 8/12/41

Yes, My Darling Daughter DR 5774 DeE F7876, BrSA 1926, DeE RFLD39
Emp RAJCD815 w. Doreen Villiers & Amb & his orch 21/5/41

Yesterday's Dream DR5202 DeE F7695 w.Amb & his Orch 30/12/40

Yes, You Were Right DR15930 DeE F9692, Lon.1052 w. the Johnston
Brothers & Robert Farnon & his orch 12/3/51

You and I DR6335 DeE F7993 w. Amb & his orch. 8/10/41

You'd be so Nice to Come Home To DR7373 DE F8327, ACL1186,
Jas.JASM2017, GNP9004 Fla PAST CD7048 w. Amb & his orch
19/6/43

You'll Never Know DR7378-2 DeE F8328 ASV CD AJA5150 AS unn. w.
Amb & his orch 1/7/43

You Say the Sweetest Things, Baby DR5400 DeE F7771, BrSA 1882 w.
Ambrose & his Orch 27/2/41

You're Breaking My Heart All Over Again DR5269 DeD F7705, BrSA1877
s.Amb & his Orch 17/1/41

You're in My Arms DR6424 DeE F8027 NX 8.120663 Voc CDEA6096 w.
Ambrose & his orch. 12/11/41

You're Not Living in Vain PHI PB969 BBE12344 SFMR 5MCD624

You Rhyme With Everything that's Beautiful DR7450 DeE F8344 Fla
PAST CD7048 Peg PGN CD821 w. Amb & his orch 29/7/43

You, Too, Can have a Lovely Romance DR7340 DeE F8316 w. orch acc
20/5/43

You've Changed DR11834-2 DeE F8907, SPA140, Lon 118 Fla PAST
   CD7850 Voc CDEA6036 MFP CD-DL1263 w. orch directed by
   Camarata 28/11/47
You Walk By DR7033 DeE F8221 w. orch acc. 14/10/42
You Were Never Lovelier DR7812-2 DeE F8282 w. Ambrose & his orch
   11/2/43
Yours R6347-1 Rex 10068 Flare ROYCD239 w. Jay Wilbur's orch 10/10/41

Jo Shelton (Anne's Sister)

If There Are Stars in My Eyes AS ASCD01
I Need Your Arms Around Me AS unn
More Romancing AS unn
Tread Softly AS unn (Special dubbing duet with Anne from Philips
   recording listed in main Anne Shelton discography)

LPS

Decca

RECDL1 *British Dance Bands of the 4s* (w. Ambrose - others Lew Stone,
   Oscar Rbin 7 Royal Air Force Dance Orchestra)
RECDL3 *Starlight Serenades - Four Vocalists of the 40s* (with Vera
   Lynn, Denny Dennis, Donald Peers) #
RFL10 *Ambrose & His Orchestra* (with other artists)
RFL41 *Anne Shelton Sings With Ambrose & His Orchestra* Jasmine
   JASM2017 *Ambrose Tribute To Cole Porter* (with other artists)

London (USA)

Anne Shelton Favorites London (USA) LPB59
Anne Shelton Favorites Vol 2 London (USA) LB707

Music For Pleasure (EMI)

MFP 41 1048 3 *The Magic of Anne Shelton* (2 LP Set)

Phillips & Phillips International

PHI431 *Irish Souvenirs*
BBL7291 *Songs from the Heart*

Wing (Philips)

WL1080 (B 10727) L *Anne Shelton - My Heart Sings*

World Record Club

T832 *Anne Shelton Showcase*

EP

Decca

DFE6321 *Four Standards*

Phillips

BBE12218 *Anne Shelton*

BBE12292 *Just Love Me*

BBE12344 *Songs of Faith*

BBE12900 *Anne Shelton*

BBE12169 *The Shelton Sound*

BBE12205 (425 052 BE) *The Italian Touch*

BBE12347 (SBBE9003) *My Yiddishe Momma*

BBE12340 *Favourites*

433.635BE *There's No Song Like An Irish Song*

433.636BE *When Irish Eyes Are Smiling*

CD

Anne Shelton (Special Label by Kelly Richards – Anne & Jo Shelton's Niece)

ASCD01 *Thank You Captain Miller*

ASCD02 *My Pal Jo.*

AJA5150 *Anne Shelton – The Early Years*

AJA5163 *Living Era V-E Day 50ʰ Anniversary The Musical Memories* (with other artists)

AJS286 *Forces Sweethearts & Heart Throbs of WWII* (with other artists – 2 CD)

PNACD001 *Poppy Memories* (with other artists)

Castle

PBX CD422 *The Great British Dance Bands* (with other artists – 4 CD Set)

PBX447/1-4 *The Great British Dance Bands & Their Vocalists* (with other artists – 4 CD Set)

Conifer

CDHD301 *Wish Me Luck As You Wave Me Goodbye – Popular Songs of the War Years* (with other artists)

EMI

CBP 7 94763 2 *Anne Shelton*

Empress

RAJCD845 *VE Day – The Vocalists* (with other artists)

RAJCD815 *Anne Shelton Sings with Ambrose & his Orchestra*

RAJCD875 *Vocalists – Recollections of 1945* (with other artists)

Flapper (Pearl)

PAST CD7048 *A Nightingale sang in Berkely Square* – Anne Shelton

PAST CD7850 *Anne Shelton – The Velvet Touch*

Flare

ROY CD239 *Sweet Songbirds* (with other artists – 2CD)

Music For Pleasure (EMI)

CD-DL1269 *The Lights Can Go On Again* (with other artists 2 CD Set)

CD-DL1263 *In The Land of Beginning Again* (with other artists – 2 CD's)

Naxos

8.120663 *Anne Shelton Fools Rush In – The Early Years 1940-1941*

Past Perfect

PPPCD1300 *Christmas Spell* (with other artists)

Pegasus

PGN CD821 *Memory Lane Presents - Anne Shelton – Kiss the Boys Goodbye*

River Productions

RR CD229/231 *Songs That Won The War* (with other artists – 3 CD's)

See For Miles Records

C5MCD624 *Now Hear This – Anne Shelton*

Universal Spectrum

544-256-2 *The Best of Anne Shelton*

544 267-2 *Anne Shelton Blitz Hits*

544 427-2 *Hits of the Blitz* (with other artists)

Vocalion

CDEA6036 *Anne Shelton – In The Still Of The Night*

CDEA6072 *Lullaby of Broadway – Ambrose & His Orchestra -The Decca Years Vol 5* (with other artists)

CDEA6081 *Music! Music! Music!*

CDEA6096 *As Time Goes By – Ambrose & His Orchestra Vol 6* (with other artists)

CDEA6108 *Serenade - Ambrose & His Orchestra – The Decca Years Volume 8* (with other artists)

CDLK4199 *Merry Christmas with the Stars* (with other artists)

CDLK4198 *Ted Heath and Friends* (with other artists)

** *There Goes That Song Again* - CD cover states matrix DR7245 Decca F8291 (rec February 1943 with orchestral accompaniment) which have no record of unless this is a previously unknown version?

BrSA = Brunswick South Africa

DeE = European Decca

DeSA = Decca, South Africa

Lon = London USA